BE
THE
Parent

BE
THE
Parent

Seven Choices
You Can Make
to Raise
Great Kids

Kendra Smiley
with JOHN SMILEY

MOODY PUBLISHERS
CHICAGO

Cover Design: Koechel Peterson & Associates
Cover Image: Norbert Schaefer/Corbus
Edited by Ali Childers

Library of Congress Cataloging-in-Publication Data

Smiley, Kendra, 1952-
    Be the parent : 7 choices you can make to raise great kids / Kendra Smiley.
        p. cm.
    Includes bibliographical references.
    ISBN-13: 978-0-8024-6941-0
    1. Parent and child—Religious aspects—Christianity. 2. Parenting—Religious aspects—
Christianity. 3. Child rearing—Religious aspects—Christianity. I. Title.

  BV4529.S478 2006
  248.8'45--dc22

                                                                              2005026401

ISBN: 0-8024-6941-8
ISBN-13: 978-0-8024-6941-0

We hope you enjoy this book from Moody Publishers. Our goal is to provide high-quality, thought-provoking books and products that connect truth to your real needs and challenges. For more information on other books and products written and produced from a biblical perspective, go to www.moodypublishers.com or write to:

Moody Publishers
820 N. LaSalle Boulevard
Chicago, IL 60610

5 7 9 10 8 6 4

Printed in the United States of America

To Matthew, Aaron, and Jonathan—
The three responsible for making us parents

Contents

Acknowledgments

This has been a delightful project for me, partially because the person who deserved his name on the front of *every* book I've written now joins me as the author. "With John Smiley" is an understatement. I can honestly say that the joy and success I have experienced as an author and a parent is largely because of the love and wisdom of my partner in those endeavors. Big thanks to my husband, John.

Thanks to our adult children (three sons by birth and two daughters by marriage) for their encouragement, their wit, and their wisdom. Their loving direction as adults has helped me to communicate more accurately and compassionately. Thank you—Matthew and Marissa, Aaron and Kristin, and Jonathan.

Thanks to my parents and my parents-in-law who

gave us life and created our "normal," which had some definite positives.

Thanks to Kevin Howells, my manager, who came into our lives right on schedule. His insight, enthusiasm, professionalism, and encouragement have been a blessing to my writing, my speaking, and my family. Kevin, your unselfish assistance has allowed me to serve God in areas I would have never imagined. You have expanded my ministry.

Thanks to my friends at MOODY . . . especially to my editors, Peg Short and Ali Childers, and also to my publicist, Janis Backing. Ladies, you are some of my favorites! Thanks, too, to so many others who have made my association with MOODY a blessing.

Thanks to MOODY Publishers and to FAMILY LIFE TODAY who cosponsored the research for this project. Thanks for believing in this book and for trusting us to carry out the mission of writing it.

I have often pondered the amazing fact that God has chosen me to do so many tasks that I have enjoyed so much. Being a wife and a mother and a speaker and an author—these have all been wonderful assignments from Him. "Thanks be to God for his indescribable gift!" (2 Corinthians 9:15) Thanks be to God for Jesus. I pray that this work may glorify Him and bless the families whose lives it touches.

And now . . .

A Good Word from John —The Resident Dad

I would first like to thank God for giving me the opportunity to be a parent. At times it has been tiring and frustrating, but for the most part it has been a time of wonderful exhilaration. The task of parenting Matthew, Aaron, and Jonathan has been the most gratifying and fulfilling experience in my life so far. Thank you, Jesus.

Secondly, I would like to thank Kendra. She is the mother who gave up a very rewarding and enjoyable teaching career to be a full-time mom. Kendra brought love, laughter, and just plain fun into our home. She taught us all how to love other people. Thank you, Kendra, for being home when I was gone and for loving me when I wasn't too lovable. Thanks for using your talents as a writer to communicate these parenting principles and for allowing me to share in that process.

Thank you Matthew, Aaron, and Jonathan. You obviously made this book possible. Without you, we would have very little credibility. You three are a joy and a blessing in my life.

And finally, I want to thank my mom and dad who gave me a clear picture of the responsibilities required in parenting.

ACKNOWLEDGMENTS

Introduction

911, Emergency. May I help you?"

"Yes," the frazzled voice replied. "I'm at the grocery store and my two children have just knocked down the toilet paper display!"

"I see. Is anyone injured?"

"Oh no, that's part of the problem. Wait, I didn't mean it like that. No, nobody is injured. The kids ran away as soon as things started falling."

"So your children are lost? Is that the problem?"

"No, they're not lost. I can hear one of them in aisle three, *sorting* through the cereal. And the other one must be in the produce section. I hear falling fruit."

"Then your children are not hurt or lost?"

"No, but I am! I'm hurt by the embarrassment of

another grocery store fiasco and lost about what to do. I'm having an emergency!"

Have you been there? Have you personally experienced a grocery store fiasco filled with embarrassment and exasperation? Are you wondering if there is anything you can do to avoid repeating an incident like that again? Take heart. There is no emergency number you can phone, but you hold in your hands a powerful weapon to help you combat, and even prevent, the next emergency. Read on and become empowered to Be The Parent.

Proactive Parenting

Everyone who has ever been given the privilege and responsibility of parenting has dealt with the challenge of preparing versus reacting, of being a proactive parent rather than a reactive one. Being proactive means being prepared.

My mother was someone who lived by the Boy Scout motto, "Be prepared." This was a woman whose car had a trunk filled with emergency "necessities." There was a flashlight, a blanket, a tool kit, jumper cables, a first aid kit, and a snow shovel in the extensive inventory. Now the fact that she drove no more than six miles from home and did not drive in the snow or after dark might suggest that she was overprepared. And truthfully, even with her obsessiveness about being prepared for any and every emergency, it really could not be done.

I'm not suggesting that you carry a trunkful of supplies to combat every parental emergency that might arise. That is impossible anyway. Instead, I am challenging you to make seven choices to raise great kids. These choices have the potential to change you from a parent in turmoil to one who has the time, energy, and ability to enjoy the task at hand, the task of parenting.

Let's look back at our panicked parent. How could that grocery store scenario have been different? A proactive parent, one who has taken the initiative to make the seven choices to raise great kids, will anticipate the potential challenges in a particular setting. With that anticipation comes the establishment of boundaries, guidelines for appropriate behavior. Let me give you an idea of some helpful rules for the grocery store. Remember that children don't instinctively know the behavior boundaries for a given situation. It is important to take the time to communicate with your child beforehand.

Grocery Store Guidelines

Your child will:

1. Stay in the cart or walk beside it.

2. Walk and not run in the grocery store.

3. Select something from the shelf only if asked to do so.

4. Choose a treat *only* if this has been prearranged.

5. Understand that any infraction of these rules will result in an appropriate, predetermined punishment.

When a child knows the boundaries and respects them, you have a wonderful opportunity to praise his behavior. A trip to the grocery store can actually be a fun outing for parent and child *if* you have established reasonable guidelines *before* shopping, if you have chosen to be proactive

"But Kendra, that takes time." Correct. Proactive parenting takes time, but so does reactive parenting. And the latter typically takes not only time—it is also usually accompanied by embarrassment, anger, annoyance, frustration and exhaustion. You make the choice.

Be the Parent highlights seven intentional choices. Each choice is embodied by five action steps, with added feedback from John—the resident dad—and families who face challenges similar to yours. In sidebars throughout the book, we've included findings from an independent, national survey of hundreds of Christian parents: married, divorced, and single. These statistics reveal and confirm some of the concerns most frequently voiced in our parenting seminars.

Understanding the issues that you and other parents like you are facing, our goal is to help you learn ways to make your home life more tranquil and happy while raising great children. How can we help? By preparing you to make positive choices on a daily basis.

Let's begin with Choice #1: Choose to Be The Parent.

Choose to Be the Parent

Honey, hop into your car seat, and I'll buckle you up."

"No! I don't want to sit in my seat! I don't want to wear a seat belt! I don't want to go for a ride!"

Now what? What's a parent to do when a request is denied? What's next when an order is turned down by a four-year-old as though it was an option? What should you do if the command to "hop into your car seat" turns into World War III with your preschooler protesting loudly, kicking furiously, and swinging like a boxer? *Now what?*

Scenarios like this happen every day. Sometimes the disobedience or threatened disobedience is subtle: "I don't want to get in my seat," the youngster says calmly. "I'm tired. Do we have to go to the store today? Could we go tomorrow?"

Sometimes it is radical: "I hate my car seat," shrieks the toddler. "I hate this car! I hate *you!*"

No one wants to have her parental authority questioned. When your child's challenge is a mild one, it is upsetting. When the response is extreme, it can be devastating. You think you are failing. Your household has been turned upside down, and you feel like you are the worst parent in the entire world! Those thoughts are very real, but they are not accurate. The question is not, Who is the worst parent in the entire world? (I'd hate to judge *that* contest.) The question is, Now what?

"I am the parent. He is the child." I said those two sentences more than once as we were raising our kids. Who was I trying to convince? Probably both of us, myself and my child. Actually, it was more of a reminder—a reminder I needed when there had been a mysterious role reversal. Saying, "I am the parent. He is the child," helped me restore each one of us to our proper place.

YOU ARE NOT ALONE: OVER 1/3 OF CHRISTIAN PARENTS EXPERIENCE FREQUENT CONFLICT WITH THEIR CHILD OVER THE FOLLOWING: INTERACTIONS WITH SIBLINGS, CHORES, DISOBEYING PARENTS, AND BEDTIME/NAPTIME.

"I am the parent." Sounds simple, doesn't it? Of course I'm the parent. Obviously I'm the parent. I'm older. I'm wiser. I pay the bills. I make the decisions. I'm the one who is in charge. Well, um, maybe not *all* the time. In fact, my recollection is that the two sentences quoted above were uttered because I had momentarily abdicated the throne and was no longer in charge (or at least things were moving in that direction).

Somehow, one of my little sweeties, albeit the cunning toddler or the charming grade school boy, was taking control. Granted, he was neither qualified nor chosen to be in command, but evidently he had forgotten that he was the child and that I was the parent. And I guess I had forgotten it too! I was in the same position as the parent with the car seat protestor. An order was given and was being debated. That parent's authority was in question.

Who's in Charge?

"We have a problem in our home," the young father began as he was handed the microphone. We had just finished a strong-willed child seminar and had opened it up for questions. "We have a problem in our home," the father said. "Our four-year-old daughter is running the house. What can we do?" That was it. This dear man was obviously at the end of his rope, and the knot he was clinging to was fraying. His authority had been usurped by a very strong-willed child.

The honesty of that father must be appreciated and applauded. In the auditorium, heads nodded in affirmation, agreement, and commiseration. Confusion of the roles of parent and child is not unusual. After having addressed thousands of parents and answered numerous questions in seminars, workshops, and via email, I can attest to the fact that role reversal is a common problem.

So what is the answer?

The first step is precisely what we heard from that father: Admit it when there is a problem in need of a solution.

STEP ❶ *Admit it when a problem exists.*

"You will know the truth, and the truth will set you free."
—John 8:32

By holding this book in your hands, it would seem that you are willing to admit, or at least consider the idea, that there is room for help in some areas of parenting. Admitting that a problem exists may appear very simple. Simple, yes. Easy, not necessarily. For many, this first step is extremely difficult. It seems to be easier to ignore difficult situations, hoping that "with time things will change." Yes, things will change with time, but if you have compromised your role as the parent, the change will not be very pleasant.

God wants you to know and admit the truth. If you are to be "free," you must deal in the facts. The father we heard from at the seminar was willing to acknowledge that somehow, somewhere, for whatever reason, he was no longer functioning as the parent, as the one in charge. Perhaps that is the case in your home. Maybe you are tired or under stress in another area of your life. Sleep deprivation is one very common stressor for parents. Maybe you are a little defensive or overprotective when it comes to parenting. Maybe, for whatever reason, you feel inadequate. "The truth will set you free." What is the truth about your situation?

The car seat protestor we met at the beginning of this chapter felt self-assured enough to oppose his parent's order. Evidently there was confusion in their family about who was the parent, who was in charge. What is Step 1 for that parent? Admit it when a problem exists. Now is not the time to make excuses. Instead it is time to get help.

Help!

Until you realize your parent-child relationship can improve, it is unlikely things *will* improve. There can be no problem resolution until a problem is identified. That is precisely what I was doing when I announced that, "I am the parent. You are the child." Step 1 must be taken if any further advance is to occur. Admit it when a problem exists, and go on to Step 2.

STEP ❷ *Build your confidence.*

> *"The fruit of righteousness will be peace; the effect of righteousness will be quietness and confidence forever."*
> —Isaiah 32:17

If Step 2 is to build your confidence, it might be appropriate to determine how it eroded in the first place. Many times losing a simple skirmish will trigger the wearing away of a parent's confidence. When you pick a battle, you must win.

Dad is in the local pizza parlor with a group of friends. His child has finished eating, but the group as a whole is not done. Little Hannah starts to squirm in her chair, and Dad tells her to stay seated. Almost before the words leave his mouth, she jumps down and walks around the table to visit with one of the other adults. "Is this really so bad?" Dad asks himself. "She isn't running around or causing a commotion." So he lets it go and doesn't reinforce the instruction that was given.

Is it a big deal for this youngster to leave her seat and walk around the table? No. Is it a big deal to willfully disobey an instruction from her parent? Yes! Dad just lost a battle he chose to fight. His confidence is potentially disintegrating and so is his child's respect for him. It's important to think about your commands before you give them. Pick your battles wisely.

When you choose a particular battle to fight, when you draw a line in the sand, it is essential that you win. The dad in the pizza parlor told his daughter to stay seated. The mother told her son to get into the car seat. These were not points of discussion or items to debate. The children were not asked if they would *like* to obey.

When an order is given, there is never a debate. And because there is no question, it is important that you give your orders wisely. The little girl must stay seated. The little boy must get into his car seat. If once or twice your child has been allowed to "win the battle," then he has learned that the orders given are debatable. Your authority and confidence are in jeopardy.

If losing daily skirmishes can tear down the confidence of a parent, what will build it up? The obvious: winning the daily skirmishes. Also a parent's confidence may be bolstered by something as simple as doing a reality check.

IT'S A TOUGH JOB: 70% OF CHRISTIAN PARENTS ADMIT THAT THEY SOMETIMES LACK CONFIDENCE IN THEIR PARENTING DECISIONS.

Too often, parents have given up their rights and responsibilities because they have lost track of what is truly reality. That four-year-old darling who had taken over the house had managed, consciously or unconsciously, to convince the adults that they were not capable of being the parents. She had persuaded them that she was better equipped to be in charge, and obviously, she was more than willing. The preschooler who was not interested in following the instruction to get into his car seat and buckle up was also questioning his parent's authority. The pizza parlor prowler completely ignored the words of her father.

These kids had taken charge or were threatening to do so. So what reality does a parent need to examine to build his confidence? It is the reality that your child is not prepared cognitively, experientially, or emotionally to be the one in control. No child has the skills needed to Be The Parent.

Perhaps the best illustration of this is one that borders on the ridiculous. Imagine riding in the car with your preschooler and taking turns at the wheel. You drive for a while and then hop out of the driver's seat and he takes over. Good idea? *Of course not!* He's only three! He doesn't have the skills to drive a car. He can't even reach the pedals. No parents would give control of their automobile to their child. Then why give your child control of parenting, a role that the child is not capable of handling? This decision could be equally destructive.

Snap back to reality! It is NEVER best to allow your child to control your household. Beyond a shadow of a doubt, you are better equipped for the job of being in charge. Your confidence level should be raised just by doing a reality check.

Back to reality

Please repeat after me . . .
I am the parent . . . THAT is reality.
He (or she) is the child . . . THAT is reality.
I am older and wiser . . . THAT is reality.

God has given me the parenting
    responsibility . . . THAT is reality.
He will equip me to do the job . . .
    THAT is realty.
I can have God-given confidence in
    my role . . . THAT is reality.
I am the parent!

If it is your goal to Be The Parent, you must choose to, Step 1: Admit it when a problem exists; Step 2: Build your confidence (with a heavy dose of reality); and . . .

STEP ❸ *See the vision.*

> *"Where there is no vision, the people perish."*
> —Proverbs 29:18 KJV

God gave Adam and Eve, the first earthly parents, a twofold task as they started their life together in the garden. He told them to, "Be fruitful and increase in number; fill the earth and subdue it" (Genesis 1:28). Complying with the first part of that instruction was not difficult then, and it is not difficult today. Becoming a parent, conceiving a child, being fruitful and increasing in number—that is usually the easy part. The difficulty comes with subduing that fruit! Therefore, it is important to have a vision. A vision will help you keep your focus. It will help you from being shortsighted.

A Vision?

What is your vision for your child? I am NOT talking about deciding that little Jimmy, only five years old, will one day be the pianist of the London Philharmonic Orchestra. I am not suggesting you declare that particular intent and then go after it with abandon even if little Jimmy hates the piano and has absolutely no musical ability. That is not what I mean when I challenge you to have a vision. A vision, as I am referring to it in this case, is more general and overarching. It is not a future career goal or a benchmark of society. It is not you desiring for your child to become what you have become or achieve what you have achieved. Nor is it expecting that your child become or achieve what you have not.

Let me share the vision my husband and I had for each one of our sons. We wanted to help our children "sing the song God put inside of them." This is the type of overarching goal or vision any parent can adopt. That was the vision we saw for our boys.

Seeing the vision for your child is akin to the concept presented in *Experiencing God* by Henry Blackaby and Claude King. The reader is encouraged to find where God is *already* at work and come alongside Him.

> God is a sovereign ruler of the universe. He is the One who is at work, and He alone has the right to take the initiative to begin a work. He does not ask us to dream our dreams for Him and then ask Him to bless our plans. He is already at work when He comes to us. His desire is to get us from where we are to where He is working. When God reveals to you where He is working, that becomes His invitation to join Him.[1]

Where is God working in your child's life? What skills and interests and abilities has He given your son or daughter?

Identify these and get in step to enhance them and to help your child "sing his song."

Their Song

The vision we had for each of our sons was to help them "sing the song God put inside of them." That was the way we worded it. We did not set out to help them sing "our song," or the song *we* determined they must sing. "Train a child in the way *he should go*" (Proverbs 22:6, emphasis mine). Each one of our three sons was and is very different. How can three boys with the same parents, the same grandparents, living in the same community, attending the same church, all be so different? Because that is what God intended. If our Creator can make each snowflake an original, I'm certain that creating every human being to be unique is in the realm of His ability.

Unique

"For you created my inmost being; you knit me together in my mother's womb. I praise you because I am fearfully and wonderfully made."
—Psalm 139:13–14

That verse is the beautiful, poetic explanation of each person's individuality. My sons used a more humorous approach. "Mom always reminds people that they are unique —just like everyone else!" Yes, we are all different, all unique, and each one of your children and mine is an individual. So how did we go about accomplishing this vision? We had to carefully observe our boys and get to know them as individuals. We had to listen to their dreams, their fears, and their ideas—starting when they were very young.

Listening takes time—time alone with each child and time together as a family. We took the time to work together and to play together. But it isn't just time; it's listening too. You must listen as your child expresses himself. Too many times, parent-child dialogue is actually parent-driven monologue. And usually that monologue sounds like a list of dos and don'ts, like an instruction manual. "Don't do that. Do this." We already live in a noisy world. You will have to make a conscious choice to listen to your child.

The Five-Day Challenge

So how can you be intentional when it comes to communication with your child? Take the five-day challenge. Announce that for the next five days, the car is not only going to be a transportation vehicle but is going to become the place for conversation. All distractions: cell phones, DVD players, CDs, the radio are forbidden, outlawed for five whole days! The only sounds allowed within the confines of the automobile will be those of the driver and passengers engaged in conversation! This will be a chore for most families who have found these distractions very convenient. They may be convenient, but they definitely stifle communication. The challenge is to turn off the distractions for five days and connect with your family. You will need to ask open-ended questions to begin the conversation. For example:

1. Tell me about your favorite piece of playground equipment. Why do you like it? Do you think I would like it?

2. What is one color you really like? Can you guess what my favorite color is? Why do you think I like that one?

3. Do you have a favorite song?

4. Can you remember the Bible story from last week's Sunday school lesson? Did you learn a Bible verse this week?

The questions do not need to highlight monumental things. The point is to converse. Be a listener and be willing to share. Obviously the questions will change as the age of your child changes. There were times when we made the conversation into a guessing game.

"Who was in Sunday school today?" I would ask.

"Try to guess," was the answer.

And then I would guess various names (some legitimate, some silly) and our conversation was fun and lively.

Take the five-day challenge anytime you feel that communication has been stymied. Pay attention and you will actually hear what your child is thinking and dreaming. The better listener you become, the better opportunity you have to help your child determine the song that God placed within him— and the more likely you are to see the vision come to life!

Being able to see the vision for each one of your children is an important part of proactive parenting. Just as it is important for the mother of our original car seat protester to admit that she needs help, and to build her confidence through a reality check, she must see the vision for her child. As this mother strives to help her son sing his song, she will have increased determination to calmly and confidently win the battles she has chosen. This mother can be certain of the value of restoring and maintaining peace. By being the parent, she will ensure that the time she and her son have together will not be wasted in useless, disrespectful chaos but will instead be positive and productive.

And there is more. We have just begun to develop the choices to be made for proactive parenting. Step 1: Admit it when a problem exists; Step 2: Build your confidence; Step 3: See the vision. And now you must have a plan.

STEP ④ *Develop a plan.*

> *"In his heart a man plans his course, but the LORD determines his steps."*
> —Proverbs 16:9

Naively, some new parents assume that they automatically possess all the skills and knowledge needed to be parents simply because they now have a little one in their home. After all, the new parents had parents of their own. Surely they learned something from their folks. And if their parents made mistakes, as they undoubtedly did, these have been identified and can now be avoided. It's easy . . . isn't it?

Well, what if you didn't have two parents in your home? What if you had a parent who was present but who was emotionally absent or incapable of good parenting for whatever reason? A man told me that when he came to a parenting emergency, he would step back and ask, "What did my father do in a situation like this?" Unfortunately the answer was, "Get drunk." Not an option.

This is an extreme example. But maybe one or both of your parents were inaccessible because of their work schedule or their interest, maybe even obsession, with the television, the newspaper, their own friends, or simply the desire to nap. Just remembering how your parents did it is not enough.

In a perfect world, your parents gave you a good supply of parenting tools to use with your own children. Maybe your spouse's parents did the same. It is possible that you both feel well equipped. (After all, look at how delightful you two turned out!) However, even if both of you had positive, confident, proactive parents, you bring different biases and routines into your new family. I'm guessing that your two families of origin, the families where you and your spouse were raised, did some things differently.

Are you aware of the definition of *normal*? It is whatever YOUR family did (regardless of how bizarre it might have been). You and your spouse bring two different "normals" that will contribute to the creation of the new "normal" for your family unit. (Which, by the way, someday your child's spouse will question, "You think *that* is normal?")

Furthermore, your parents did not raise this child of yours . . . this unique individual who God has given you. All that is to say that whether or not the parenting you and your spouse received was superlative, you still need to be proactive and have a plan to help your child develop into a responsible adult with well-placed priorities. Here's how to help your child "sing his song":

1. Give your child the opportunity to know Jesus.

"Let the little children come to me, and do not hinder them, for the kingdom of God belongs to such as these."
—Mark 10:14

What do proactive parents do to see that their children know and love the Lord? There are opportunities you can give your child to become a member of the family of God. You can be intentional in seeing that the child in your home develops a relationship with Christ—and the sooner the better. No parent can make a child accept Christ as his or her Savior. There are, however, certain things a parent can do that can encourage that personal decision.

First of all, your commitment to Christ is of utmost importance (see the appendix: "The Plan of Salvation"). Your child is watching you and listening too. Even when your child is young, he will be deciding if you are the "real deal." This shouldn't panic you, and this is not a call to perfection. It is a reflection of the attitude of your heart. If having your child know Christ is truly important to you, this will be reflected in your behavior.

Be sure to find a church where the gospel is preached, children are loved, and Christian growth is encouraged. Then joyfully engage in opportunities to serve as individuals and as a family.

2. Teach your child to obey.

"Children, obey your parents in the Lord, for this is right."
—Ephesians 6:1

Teaching your child to obey you and helping him realize there are consequences for disobedience are two things that are essential. These will encourage your child's ability and willingness to obey God. This is the essence of choosing to Be The Parent.

A parent understands that boundaries are important. God gives us boundaries—not to fence us in—to protect us from the perils outside of the parameters. Your responsibility as the parent is to determine —and reinforce— those boundaries.

Routine

Children thrive on routine. In one sense, routine provides boundaries. Your child needs a consistent schedule. What time does his day begin? When is bedtime? Mealtime is another activity that needs to be predictable. Putting your child on a schedule, creating those boundaries, has many benefits. Routine provides assurance of parental care. "I know we will be having lunch at noon . . . I know Mommy and Daddy put me to bed at 8:00 p.m. each evening . . . We do this every day." There is a feeling of safety with boundaries.

And there is also freedom. A child who realizes where the boundaries are located, and heeds them, is able to run free within those boundaries. A child without reinforced boundaries does not have the freedom or safety he needs. Boundaries are not limited to routines. As the parent, you need to communicate to your child the acceptable behavior for various settings—church, the grocery store, the automobile, to name a few. There are boundaries in regard to certain people groups. What is the appropriate response to a teacher, a babysitter, a grandparent? When your child knows the boundaries and you have reinforced the appropriate behavior of staying within those boundaries, he can be confident in those settings. He knows what is expected and what to expect from you.

Many times kids act up to get attention. Even if the attention is negative, they have decided it is better than being ignored. Be sure you are giving your child the attention and positive reinforcement that he needs. Our mom with the anti-car-seat son will want to be sure her son:

1. complies with the order she has given, and then . . .

2. is rewarded with as much positive attention as Mom can safely give as they head down the highway.

Active parenting is important as your child relates to you within the boundaries. Let me give you another example. Since we started with the grocery store, let's continue there. When you are shopping with your child, do not ignore him. Include him in the process. It is not all about efficiency. It is about having positive interaction with your child. The grocery store can be an adventure in learning and in enjoying one another. For example, you can ask a child for help in finding a particular product. I said "finding a product" not pulling it off of the shelf. Your child should not take anything from a shelf or a display unless you have asked him to do so. When he follows your instruction, he is your helper not a hindrance.

In an age-appropriate fashion, you can talk about the various food products and nutrition and agriculture and more. The possibilities for learning are limitless! Your child is getting attention within prescribed boundaries, and you are enjoying your child *and* getting the grocery shopping finished with a smile on your face.

Being the parent means teaching your child to obey. That is not being cruel. It is being biblical, knowing that with obedience comes freedom. Let me say it one more time. Being the parent means teaching your child to obey.

If you make a commitment to these two objectives, to giving your child the opportunity to know Jesus and to teaching him to obey, you will be well on your way to success as a parent. Those are a part of the plan.

Now you have seen four of the action steps. You understand how important it is to: Step 1: Admit it when a problem exists; Step 2: Build your confidence; Step 3: See the vision; Step 4: Develop a plan. There is only one more step.

STEP ❺ *Know you will make mistakes, and keep on learning.*

"Let the wise listen and add to their learning, and let the discerning get guidance."
—Proverbs 1:5

There is no perfect parent. In fact, if you ask any seasoned parent, "Did you always make the right choices?" the honest ones will have to admit that many of their good choices were the result of experience gained from making poor ones. We made mistakes in parenting. You have made mistakes in parenting. That is OK. Do not let those mistakes paralyze you.

Being the parent will allow you the opportunity to make mistakes and to ask for forgiveness. The idea is NOT to repeat the same mistakes over and over. To *learn* as a parent means a change of behavior. The goal is to keep learning and becoming a better parent. And to accomplish that you must Choose to Be The Parent!

A Good Word from John —The Resident Dad

Kendra is 100 percent correct when she says that the first step in proactive parenting is to admit that a

ACTION STEPS:

STEP ❶ Admit the problem exists.

STEP ❷ Build your confidence.

STEP ❸ See the vision.

STEP ❹ Develop a plan.

STEP ❺ Know you will make mistakes, and keep on learning.

problem exists. If that is sometimes difficult for a mom to do, it is incredibly *difficult for a dad. We dads like to believe we are in charge and that our children could not possibly be usurping our position. Furthermore, we absolutely do not want to think that others might have noticed that we are losing control.*

I have seen situations where it is obvious that the child and the parent have reversed roles. The dad appears to be clueless and makes excuses if and when any attention is drawn to the apparent problem. This is sad for both parent and child.

There is a quick test you can do to see if you might have a problem being the parent. Choose the correct answer that is the closest match.

When I give my child a direction, he:

> a) *ignores my instruction.*
> b) *argues with me.*
> c) *throws a fit.*
> d) *does what I have asked.*

If your answer is a, b, or c, take note. The possibility exists that there has been a role reversal. Don't be afraid to admit the problem exists. That is the loving, parental thing to do.

One more note from Kendra:
Be The Parent, Not the Friend

There is one more problematic role sometimes assumed by parents that I want to address before we move on to the next choice. Many parents try to be a friend to their child instead *of being the parent. Being a friend to your adult child is both appropriate and necessary if you are to have a relationship, for very few adults are in need of a "mommy" or "daddy." If, however, you are currently in the throes of parenting and your child has not yet reached adulthood, do not, I repeat, do not try to be a friend to your child. Your child probably has many friends in his or her age group. Which, by the way, is* NOT *your age group. Look in the mirror. You are old! I don't care if you are only twenty-five years old, you are old in comparison to your child! While your child may have an abundance of friends, it is highly unlikely that many are clamoring for the job of parent. That is your role. Be The Parent.*

> **62% OF CHRISTIAN PARENTS SAY THEIR CHILDREN CONSIDER THEM THEIR BUDDIES. *IF THAT'S HOW THEY PRIMARILY SEE YOU, THERE IS A PROBLEM.***

Note:
1. Henry T. Blackaby and Claude V. King, *Experiencing God* (Nashville: Broadman and Holman, 1994), 35.

Choose to Be a Role Model

Kendra, our store is sponsoring a fashion show, and we'd like you to be one of the models."

Now before you get all excited and flip to the back cover picture on this book in disbelief, let me tell you even more about how astounding this invitation was. I am five foot four and a half inches tall. (I began noting that half-inch as I witnessed my own mother shrinking.) I have never been described as *svelte*. It's more like "not too bad for a woman over fifty who gave birth to three." The last time I can remember my dress size in single digits was when I wore a girls' 6X. Do you understand why I was amazed by this request?

"You'd like *me* to model? I don't know if that's a good idea. I've never done anything like that before."

"Really, Kendra, it's easy. All you have to do is look elegant, and you don't have to say a word."

I should have known right then and there to say no. I could not list either looking elegant or not saying a word as my *forte*. But I didn't follow my instincts, and I said yes to modeling. It was a once in a lifetime experience—*Kendra Smiley, runway model.*

Another Model

Several years ago, a television interview made it very clear. "I am *not* a role model," proclaimed Charles Barkley, professional basketball star. Hmmm . . . another reticent model. Evidently, he was even less enthused than I was about modeling. Was his public disclaimer adequate? Did it remove him from the ranks or the responsibilities of a role model? The answer is easy. No, it did not. While I could have chosen not to partake in the modeling opportunity offered by the dress store, even if I said no, I could not opt out of being a role model. And Charles Barkley could not opt out of being a role model either. Mom and Dad, neither can you.

Since that is the case, the title for this chapter is not 100 percent accurate. You cannot choose whether or not you will be a role model for your kids. You *are* a role model. Instead, the choice is whether you will be a positive role model or a negative one. That is the first step . . .

STEP ❶ *Know that, for better or worse, you are a role model.*

"Therefore I urge you to imitate me."
—1 Corinthians 4:16

Imitation is the highest form of flattery, at least that's how the saying goes. With your children, imitation has more to do with modeling than with flattery. Years ago my brother-in-law tore his Achilles tendon. After surgery, the rehabilitation process was lengthy, taking close to a year. Walking without a limp was almost impossible. Before long his son was limping too. Consciously or unconsciously, he was imitating his dad. No encouragement was necessary because the imitation was natural.

So whether or not you are eager to join Paul in his statement in 1 Corinthians 4 to urge others to imitate you, your child *will* imitate you. You are a role model, even if it is by default. That is why moving on to Step 2 is so important. You must . . .

STEP ❷ *Take the challenge to model the Best.*

"In everything set them an example by doing what is good."
—Titus 2:7

God's Word is very clear. We are instructed over and over to be a positive role model. "Do not imitate what is evil but what is good" (3 John 11).

Again, remember not to take this as a command to be perfect. Being "holy as God is holy" is where we set our aim.

The only parent who has probably not made a parenting mistake is the one whose child is still in the womb. Perfection is not possible, but that does not forfeit the opportunity and desire to be a positive role model.

GOOD NEWS!
98% OF CHRISTIAN PARENTS AGREE THAT *THEY* ARE RESPONSIBLE FOR BUILDING CHARACTER IN THEIR CHILD.

Mom and Dad, now is the time to move forward. Step 1: Know that, for better or worse, you *are* a role model; and Step 2: Take the challenge to model the Best. You are off to a good start. Now . . .

STEP ❸ *Discover that modeling is what you say and do.*

"What good is it, my brothers, if a man claims to have faith but has no deeds?"
—James 2:14

Too Busy

I still remember the day our youngest son declared that he was "too busy" to pick up his toys. *Too busy?* I thought. Where had he learned that phrase? Were they saying that on *Sesame Street*? No, he had heard the words from the lips of his own mother. That was the day I resolved to be sure I was never "too busy" for the things that were truly important, like my son. (Oh yes, and he *did* pick up his toys.)

What things are you saying that your children will imitate? As an elementary school teacher I found the first parent-teacher conferences very enlightening. Before the conferences I would think, *Why is it so difficult for Peter to use the correct verb tense? . . . Why is Sally's vocabulary so inappropriately "colorful"?* And then I would meet the parents and my questions would be answered. Your children are listening to you and imitating your words.

And Deeds

Too many times parents determine that all they have to do is instruct or "tell." The classic (and disappointing) catchphrase for this is, "Do what I say and not what I do." When the basketball star Charles Barkley made the statement, "I am *not* a role model," it simply drew attention to the role he was playing. When a parent declares that his words are to be heeded but not his actions, it merely draws attention to his actions. Parents, your children are listening, and they are watching.

On Stage

A few years ago I had a book of Christmas plays published. I had written and directed these plays for our local church. The actors were given the script, and I was there to provide the stage direction. Before the publication of these plays, the dialogue was written in the script, but I had not originally included any emotions, voice inflection, or stage cues. I *showed* the actors what I wanted them to do. They imitated my emotion, tone, and direction.

Research has shown that words alone are only a small part of what is communicated. In 1967, Professor Albert

Mehrabian determined that "55% of the message a person receives is nonverbal, 38% is based on tone, and only 7% is our actual words."[1] That is important information for you as you choose to be a positive role model. It is your talk and your walk. It is show-and-tell. And research indicates that actions trump words! When it came to the Christmas plays being performed in our church, there was no need to give these suggestions in print . . . the actors had me. And your child has you! She's watching, she's listening, and she's imitating you.

All right, you are convinced. You are willing to: Step 1: Know that, for better or worse, you *are* a role model; Step 2: Take the challenge to model the Best; and Step 3: Discover that modeling is what you say *and* do. Now let's examine some specific areas where you can be a positive role model as you . . .

STEP ❹ *Let this knowledge influence your behavior.*

"Stop doing wrong, learn to do right."
—Isaiah 1:16–17

Let's take a look at an example. What message are you sending in regard to the corporate worship of God? Let's say you tell your child that it is important to attend church to worship God. You believe the verse, "Let us not give up meeting together, as some are in the habit of doing, but let us encourage one another—and all the more as you see the Day approaching" (Hebrews 10:25). But then Sunday morning rolls around, and you are tired or you are busy. After all, Sunday is the only day you have to sleep in. Or you have been invited to attend an afternoon function, and you would have to go to early church to make it. You never go to early church, so you decide to skip church that Sunday.

Have you ever been too sick to attend church, but not too sick for an afternoon trip to the mall? Or too tired for worship, but not for Sunday afternoon football on TV? If you answered yes, is it possible that you are modeling *convenient* worship rather than *committed* worship? It doesn't matter how many times you tell your child that worship is important or how many times you give her no option about skipping church, your actions have canceled out your words.

48% OF CHRISTIAN PARENTS ADMIT THAT THEY DO NOT USUALLY ATTEND A CHURCH WORSHIP SERVICE EACH WEEK.

My husband, John (the resident dad), always reminds me, "It doesn't matter what people say; their actions and decisions will give them away." It's my guess that the habitual convenient worshiper is only fooling about worship being important. It's preempted by many other things.

Is what you are saying in line with what you are doing? What behavior(s) might you want to change knowing that your actions are shouting a message of their own?

Liar, Liar, Pants on Fire

Don't lie. This message is a good one and a simple instruction most parents give to their children. It is wrong to lie (see Leviticus 19:11). But what if after hearing that parental command time and time again, little Jane witnessed Mom telling the neighbor that Dad had to work late and wouldn't be able to attend the block party that afternoon. Hmmm, Jane knew that Dad wasn't working; he was playing golf. It didn't matter what Mom said; her decision to lie gave her away. The overall message to Jane was, "Don't lie most of the time, unless of course, you want to or need to."

What a disconnect! When a parent says one thing and does another, it is not the words that are believed. But what if the father in that example had been looking forward to playing golf, and he didn't want to go to the block party? That's fine. But it doesn't warrant a lie. "My husband will not make it to the block party." Period. No further explanation (and certainly not a lie) is warranted. The truth is the better option. It will encourage your child to be truthful with you.

But . . .

Let's go back to the convenient worshiper. If that is the pattern you are establishing in your home, it will be very simple for your child to come up with numerous, creative reasons for missing the opportunity for corporate worship. "But Kendra," you explain, "sometimes I *am* tired on Sunday morning. Sunday *is* the only morning I can sleep in!"

And what is my answer to that very honest plea for a dispensation? "It doesn't matter." Choosing to Be The Parent, choosing to be a positive role model, means choosing to be unselfish. That is the next step.

STEP ❺ *Remember, it is not all about you.*

"Rather, clothe yourselves with the Lord Jesus Christ, and do not think about how to gratify the desires of the sinful nature."
—Romans 13:14

I grew up in the home of an alcoholic. My father was a generous and kind man, a dentist, a so-called pillar of the community (whatever that is), and an alcoholic. Because of my dysfunctional home, I honed the skill of selfishness. My perception was that the adults in our home were too busy with their own conflict, and I'd better be sure I got what I wanted and needed. I had to look out for me.

This is not an excuse nor something I am proud of. It is merely reality. For the last thirty-some years since I accepted Christ as my Savior, I have worked at becoming less selfish. With the incredible miracle of conception in our sixth year of marriage, there was the unmistakable call to be a positive role model. There are times in parenting that being unselfish is almost easy. (I said *almost*.) When a hungry baby is crying in the middle of the night and must be fed, you cannot put yourself first even if you want to. But there are also plenty of opportunities to think *only* about you:

"I *am* too tired to go to church."

"I *do* want to dodge that block party . . . even if someone has to lie."

"Why do I always have to think about the impression I am making on my children? It is just too much!"

A Big Assignment

No, it's not too much. It's a big assignment, but it only lasts for about the first eighteen years of your child's life. Please hear what I am saying. I'm not suggesting that you dedicate your every breath to your child for eighteen years. I am saying that, for the parenting years, for right now when you have a young child, you need to think about your child and her needs ahead of your own. Being unselfish does not mean being an overindulgent parent. Being unselfish means that Christ is number one and your temporary assignment to parent your child is a primary task at hand. There will potentially be many years after your child reaches adulthood when you will have the freedom to, in a sense, do your own thing. While you are in the midst of parenting, you have the opportunity to set an example of unselfishness for your child.

ACTION STEPS:

STEP ❶ Know that, for better or worse, you *are* a role model.

STEP ❷ Take the challenge to model the Best.

STEP ❸ Discover that modeling is what you say *and* do.

STEP ❹ Let this knowledge influence your behavior.

STEP ❺ Remember, it is not all about you.

(Insert your name) is called to "be [an imitator] of God."
—Ephesians 5:1
"God is love."
—1 John 4:16

AND

Love . . . and (Insert your name)
. . . is patient
. . . is kind
. . . does not envy
. . . does not boast
. . . is not proud
. . . is not rude
. . . is not self-seeking
. . . is not easily angered
. . . keeps no record of wrongs
—1 Corinthians 13:4–5

A Good Word from John —The Resident Dad

There were times when we were raising our children that I wanted to rewind the tape in their memories and erase something they had seen me do or heard me say. One of the most painful ones that comes to my mind is the time when in frustration I yelled at a player from the stands at a high school football game, "Can't you catch a pass?!" Rewinding and erasing was not possible. So I had to settle for the next best alternative. I apologized to the football player, to his parents, and to our son. Yes, I modeled a bad decision, but I followed it with a good one. (And I chose not to repeat the poor choice.)

There are very few things parents do that are more *important* than being a godly role model for their children. When children are young, parents play a starring role in their lives. Your children watch you, listen to you, and want to be just like you. If Dad and Mom do it, it must be the right thing to do. If Dad and Mom say it, it must be the right thing to say. That is an ominous responsibility for the parent. Can you handle the task? Yes, you can because God sent His Son to model for you. If your goal is to learn as much as you can about your heavenly Father and to follow His example, you will be well on the way to being a good role model for your children. Will you make mistakes? Undoubtedly. You may even yell at a player at a football game and have to apologize. When that or any other bad decision occurs, you must simply make the next right choice. And then learn from the poor choice and don't repeat it.

One of my favorite biblical illustrations of Christ being a role model for us is found in Mark chapter 1. Jesus had worked very hard all day long and even into the evening. Then the next day, "very early in the morning, while it was still dark, Jesus got up, left the house and went off to a solitary place, where he prayed" (Mark 1:35). When our kids were young, I had more than one job. Many times I worked very hard all day long and even into the evening. What did Jesus do after tiring days like that? He got up early to pray. That is our model. No *excuses. Getting up early the next morning to pray was a priority for Christ. That is a lesson I finally learned. I wish I had learned it sooner.*

Jesus is the perfect model. Our challenge as parents is to learn as much as we can about Him. Our challenge is to model the characteristics of Christ.

Note:
1. Nicholas Boothman, *How to Make People Like You* (New York: Workman Publishing, 2000), 55.

CHOICE 3

Choose to Be Present

The twenty-five year debate continues. As a parent, what am I trying to achieve, quantity time with my children or quality time? No parent would argue against the importance of quality time. My idea is that it is not a question of either/or. Instead, I believe that quality time is something that occasionally occurs while you are busy having quantity time. And that leads to the first action step for the parent who is choosing to be present.

STEP ❶ *Guarantee quantity time with your child.*

"Teach them [these words of mine] to your children, talking about them when you sit at

home and when you walk along the road,
when you lie down and when you get up."
—Deuteronomy 11:19

This verse is a wonderful illustration of Step 1. It aptly covers the quantity angle by including sitting at home, walking along the road, lying down, and getting up. And, actually, Step 2 is also covered in that verse. Step 1: Guarantee quantity time with your child, and then . . .

STEP ❷ *Orchestrate quality moments in your quantity time.*

"Teach them [these words of mine] to your children, talking about them when you sit at home and when you walk along the road, when you lie down and when you get up."
—Deuteronomy 11:19, my emphasis

Being in attendance is not enough. As someone who desires to Be The Parent, you must look for ways to connect and to be truly present in the life of your child.

The Remote

A man and his remote control—now that is a relationship that is difficult for most women to understand. Being the mother of three gentlemen and the wife of one, the remote is something I very seldom possess. I just don't have it when it comes to championship-level channel changing. But I do have an idea that this highly developed skill has at least one serious drawback. The ability to control and interact with the TV screen (eliminating any un-desired scenes or commercials with very little effort) might be leading some men, some dads, to falsely believe they can control and interact with their children in the same way—by remote control. This is counter to quality time.

Moms Beware!

Now before any moms start reciting out loud the last paragraph to their husbands, let me advance another con-cept, one that will be more painful to us ladies. Mom, here's a question for you. What behavior do you value that may negatively affect your ability to guarantee quality time with your children? The answer is multitasking—doing two, three, or half a dozen things at the same time. Multitask-ing is something we women value highly, as though it was an Olympic event. In truth, I have wondered more than once if multitasking might not be a curse. It is multitasking that en-courages us to get a few phone calls done while we are driving with our kids. Multitasking allows us to cook dinner, nurse the baby, check Jodi's spelling words, and scold the dog, all at the same time. No wonder Jodi doesn't think we really care about her spelling words (or maybe even about her).

CHRISTIAN PARENTS WHO SPEND AN HOUR OR LESS A DAY INTERACTING WITH THEIR CHILDREN ARE SIGNIFICANTLY MORE LIKELY TO FEEL THAT MASS MEDIA HAS GREAT INFLUENCE OVER THEIR CHILDREN.

Dads may try to parent by remote control and lose

opportunities for quality time, but we moms try to parent as an addendum to the other urgent things of life. Both Mom and Dad may be physically present, and quantity time may be prolific. Both parents may be in the same house or even the same room as their children, but the question remains. Ask yourself, "Am I physically present but emotionally absent?"

As a parent choosing to be present, you must, Step 1: Guarantee quantity time with your child; Step 2: Orchestrate quality moments in your quantity time; and . . .

STEP ❸ *Work, play, and pray with your child.*

"For you know that we dealt with each of you as a father deals with his own children, encouraging, comforting and urging you to live lives worthy of God, who calls you into his kingdom and glory."
—1 Thessalonians 2:11–12

I saw a plaque that read, *Be good to your children. They will choose your nursing home.* What does it mean to be good to your children? The essence is found in the verse above. You are good to your children by encouraging, comforting, and urging them to live lives worthy of God. These three things take quantity time. They can be accomplished while you work, play, and pray together, but they require making an investment of time in your child. One thing I know about the investment industry is that you want to invest in something with a good return. I can't offer you a hot stock tip, but here is a parenting tip worth applying: Take time to build a relationship with your child by investing time working, playing, and praying together.

Hard at Work

Working together with your child is a great opportunity to enjoy quantity and quality time. It is important to emphasize the word *together*. I am not talking about assigning tasks to be done independently. I am suggesting that you take on everyday jobs together.

What can your child do to work with you while you cook, for example? Kids love to measure ingredients and to stir them together. All of this takes supervision, of course. I am fully aware that having a young helper will not necessarily make your tasks easier or more efficient. The goal is quality time made possible by spending quantity time together. A simple batch of cookies can be a fun activity to do together —one with a sweet reward. Our objective is to be working together, talking, learning, and sharing an experience.

CHOCOLATE CHIP COOKIES— TOGETHER

One extra package of chocolate chips for
nibbling . . . $3
More flour to replace what is
spilled . . . $ .25
Eaten cookie dough . . . $2
Time with your child . . . priceless!

How about when you do yard work? Or when you clean, do the dishes, or walk the dog? Think of work that you do and determine how you can include your child. Your child should not be an observer or be doing the dirty work. Too often a parent will assign their child the jobs that are the most difficult or the least appealing. That is not appropriate. Regardless of the age of your child (beyond infancy), there is bound to be some way your child can help.

Working together accomplishes several things. Your child is spending quantity time with you and quality time can result as you teach a skill, solve a problem, or have a conversation. Not only that, but your child will feel that he or she is a necessary part of the family. Too many children today are seen, and see themselves, as an unimportant part of the family or even a liability. Their presence creates *more* work, costs *more* money, and causes *more* stress. Be certain you are not consciously or unconsciously communicating that message to your child. Help your children identify themselves as important and necessary parts of your family.

Again, let me remind you that efficiency is not your goal. Allowing your child to work with you will not necessarily make the job go smoother or more quickly. You have a bigger goal: working together with your child and enjoying quality time in the midst of quantity time. Even those of you with Type A personalities can learn to enjoy the adventure of working with your child if that is your intention.

Can Junior Come Out and Play?

There are many parents who miss all kinds of opportunities to play with their kids. Driving your son or daughter to the Little League game and sitting in the stands is NOT playing together. Granted, you do get credit for some pretty hefty quantity time, but most of the bonding during the game is with the parent next to you on the bleachers. Take note. I'm not advocating you miss the game. After all, then you would not be able to talk about it with your child after the last pitch is thrown. Your presence communicates that your child is important and that his activities and interests are important to you.

If observing your child's activities does not constitute playing together, what does? We've all participated in one of the simplest forms: the game of peekaboo. A two-year-old may engage you in an early form of roll and catch. Make-believe is also fun—whether it is playing with baby dolls and attending pretend parties or being a superhero.

Don't forget the preschool board games of Chutes and Ladders and Candy Land. They are two all-time favorites. Will those games stimulate you intellectually? Are they intriguing and fascinating for the average adult? Does it matter? Remember Action Step 5 in the previous chapter: It's not all about you.

It is interesting to note that the parent who is present and plays with his child from the early ages on is the parent who just might get a phone call from his adult child with an invitation to "play." Make the investment when they are young.

Let Us Pray

And praying together? That can actually start as soon as your child is born. At that point it would be more like praying *over* your child, but before long your child will be able to join you in prayer. Initially, he or she will want to pray for family and friends, or maybe for a Sunday school teacher. When the child becomes older and more independent, the prayer list may include schoolteachers, classmates, and assignments.

When our children were young, we asked them what and who they wanted to include in their bedtime prayers. After a few years, they were doing the praying, and we were simply joining in agreement. And finally, their prayers at night were done independently, no parents necessary. While we were still an active part of the bedtime prayers, we established a ritual. At the end of the prayers, either John or I would say, "Mom and Dad love you lots and lots, and who loves you best?" Each and every evening, at that prompting, they would say in a loud and exuberant voice, "Jesus!" (Correct answer!) It was a routine—a predictable question with a predictable answer. It was a ritual repeated night after night after night. And it was the truth!

We also had family devotions in the morning at breakfast. Before you get the wrong impression about our family devotion time, let me tell you that I fondly referred to it as "devotion commotion." The children would arrive at the breakfast table one at a time, and they would begin to eat. When everyone was assembled, we started the devotion time. We read a Bible verse and a short story illustrating the application of that verse. Some days we expanded on the point. Other times we didn't. Then we held hands and prayed. One of my favorite memories is hearing one of the boys, after the amen was pronounced, announcing that another brother had his eyes open. Hmmm, how did he see that? Our goal in family devotions was to share the powerful Word of God so that each child could store the Word in his heart. And while that was happening, we were also enjoying one another.

ON AVERAGE, CHRISTIAN PARENTS HAVE DEVOTIONS WITH THEIR CHILD ONLY ONCE A WEEK.

Let Us Eat

I don't want to ignore mealtime prayer. At our house, the prayer at breakfast followed the meal. At lunch and dinner we prayed in a more traditional manner, before the food was eaten. We prayed at home and when we were eating out. More than once our fast-food prayers brought positive comments from other diners. Praying before your meal is one way to testify to your faith. If we were eating with others who were unaccustomed to praying before a public meal, we purposed not to embarrass them. A simple prayer was offered that drew them into the process in a positive way. "Let's pray," either John or I would say. And then we'd immediately follow the suggestion to pray with, "Dear Jesus, bless this food. Amen." Short, simple, direct, and appropriate for the setting and the company.

When you have the desire to Be The Parent, you will choose to be present and will, Step 1: Guarantee quantity time with your child; Step 2: Orchestrate quality moments in your quantity time; Step 3: Work, play, and pray with your child. And . . .

STEP ❹ *Include your child in your adult world.*

"Let the little children come to me, and do not hinder them, for the kingdom of God belongs to such as these."
—Mark 10:14

How does a child learn to behave in adult settings? He learns by being with a loving parent who has established the boundaries and is willing to escort him through the experience.

Children's church is available at many churches. This ministry can be positive for both parent and child. The parent is able to worship and focus on the service, and the child is taught an age-appropriate lesson. Eventually though, it will be time to worship together. At the church we attend, worshiping as a family occurred at an early age because no children's church existed. Initially when our preschool children sat between us in the service, we quietly amused them with drawings and designs. Although we may have missed a point or two of the three-point sermon, the kids were learning church etiquette. At a young age they understood that talking out loud was not permissible and that with a few minor distractions/amusements, church really *didn't* last all that long. They learned patience and self-control.

Patience and self-control are two attributes that will really pay off. As your child matures, he can be invited to visit your work world (if it is outside your home). Undoubtedly, there are rules of etiquette and boundaries he can learn and experience as he interacts with you and the other adults at your workplace. The experience will give him confidence in a new setting and serve him well in life.

We made the effort to see to it that our kids were as comfortable in a fancy restaurant with multiple forks in the place setting as they were tent camping and eating near a roaring fire. Experiencing both environments and learning the etiquette and boundaries of each gave the children confidence. Choose to invite your child to be present in your world and learn the guidelines, which will make him feel safe there. That is intentional parenting.

Let's review. To be present you must, Step 1: Guarantee quantity time with your child; Step 2: Orchestrate quality moments in your quantity time; Step 3: Work, play, and pray with your child; Step 4: Include your child in your adult world; and finally . . .

STEP ⑤ *Be available for your older child, but don't interrupt him.*

"Let the wise listen and add to their learning."
—Proverbs 1:5

This may sound like a confusing action step. What does it actually mean to be available and not interrupt? Perhaps an example will illustrate it best.

Game Day

My husband, John, and I were student ministry leaders in our church for over twenty years. (Don't do the math. It's frightening.) One of the most popular excursions we took was to game day at the university about one hour away. It was sponsored by the Fellowship of Christian Athletes and featured music, testimonies, and T-shirts prior to a football game. One year we opened the event to any high school student who was interested, and we had over thirty-five students who ordered tickets to the event. With our increased number, I made a plea for adult drivers. How many volunteer drivers do you think I got? Did I have to turn some of the adults away or hold a lottery to see who would win the privilege of driving to the event? No. I drove. John drove. The two other leaders each drove and an elderly couple from the church drove a car. Oh yes. And one mother volunteered. I was sad when I realized how many parents had chosen not to invest in the quantity time of that day. Most were not willing to take the time to volunteer to spend a day with their teenager and his or her friends. They missed an opportunity for quantity and maybe even quality time.

When you drive a carload of kids, teens or otherwise, to an event, as long as you are quiet and don't interrupt, you discover a vast amount of information. What is of interest to this group? Are they boy crazy or girl crazy or sports crazy? Do they have an interest in spiritual things? How do they talk to one another? Are they respectful or teasing? When you are available and willing to serve as the chauffer and do not interrupt, before long you become invisible. From your invisible state, you can be a student of your own child and of his peers. It is an invaluable position of great benefit to a parent. You are offering service not companionship. Try it. Being available for your older child but not interrupting is the positive action of a parent who chooses to be present.

ACTION STEPS:

STEP ❶ Guarantee quantity time with your child.

STEP ❷ Orchestrate quality moments in your quantity time.

STEP ❸ Work, play, and pray with your child.

STEP ❹ Include your child in your adult world.

STEP ❺ Be available for your older child, but don't interrupt him.

A Good Word from John —The Resident Dad

As an air force reserve pilot, I flew two or three sorties a week and had a unit training assembly one weekend per month. The base where I was stationed was 110 miles from our home. On those weekend assemblies, I can remember debating about whether or not to spend Saturday night at the base. Many of the men chose to play golf after work on Saturday and then stay in the officers' quarters. If I drove home, I had to get up very early on Sunday to return to the base. Was being home with my family for a few hours on Saturday evening worth the effort? Even as I pondered that question, I knew the answer. It would have been easier to stay at the base. It would have been fun to play a round of golf after work. But being home with my family, being present, was almost always the better choice.

As parents, there are numerous convenient, fun, seemingly innocuous things that entice us to make decisions that are not in the best interest of our children. Being present requires time. Being present requires unselfishness. Being present requires effort and thinking about how we will spend each hour of the day.

Many dads, and some moms too, are prone to think that working hard and making money are legitimate substitutes for being present. After all, if you work extra hours, you will have extra money to buy things for your family. And truthfully, adults like those things too, perhaps even more than the children do. Not to mention the fact that it is sometimes easier to work outside the home than it is to be there, present with your children.

Several years ago, I read a sad letter a father had written to his son. It was like the song "Cat's in the Cradle," but a real-life embodiment. The father apologized for being absent when his son was growing up and expressed hope that they could begin a relationship now as adults. This father had mistakenly thought a big house in the city, a ski lodge in the mountains, and several fancy cars would be adequate replacements for his time. Dad had accumulated lots of things but had lost his son.

Taking time, being present to work, play, and pray is time invested wisely. Do not be distracted. Do not be shortsighted. Do not fool yourself into believing anything can take your place in the life of your child. And please, do not be selfish. Your child's success and well-being may *depend on it, and I'm certain your relationship with your adult child* will.

CHOICE 1

Choose to Be an Encourager

I taught elementary school for several years before we began our family. Almost without exception, I collectively referred to my students as "ladies and gentlemen." That might sound strange when you learn that they were no older than twelve. Why did I choose to address them this way? Weren't they boys and girls? I suppose they were if you're referring to physical maturity, but I was more interested in their behavior. I had learned that it was possible for a sixth grader or even a fourth grader to respond like a lady or a gentleman. I could encourage that mature response by my subtle suggestion. So my students were called ladies and gentlemen, and they usually rose to that expectation.

Self-fulfilling Prophecy

Expectations are interesting things. I recall hearing about a study done on male inmates in a state penitentiary. When asked how many of them had heard the phrase, "You're going to end up in jail someday," the response was overwhelming. The great majority had been told over and over again that they were destined for the penitentiary! That was the powerful expectation. Some might call it a self-fulfilling prophecy, with the idea being that these men heard it so often, they consciously or unconsciously made it happen. What are your expectations for your son or daughter?

61% OF CHRISTIAN PARENTS ADMIT THAT THEY SOMETIMES FAIL TO MOTIVATE THEIR CHILD IN POSITIVE WAYS.

The Terrible Twos

How many times have you heard about the terrible twos or the turbulent teens? Yes, those are times of significant physical, social, and intellectual changes in the lives of most individuals. But the adjectives *terrible* and *turbulent* give all the wrong implications. Do we want our children to experience a life stage that is either *terrible* or *turbulent*? Of course not. How about the expectation of the *terrific* twos or the *tremendous* teens? Does that sound like a marketing ploy? Well, maybe it is. It's an attempt to raise the expectation on those stages of development. You do not *have to* experience the negative. It is not a Scriptural mandate. I suggest that instead you . . .

STEP ❶ *Aim high, but not beyond the sky.*

"Man looks at the outward appearance, but the LORD looks at the heart."
—1 Samuel 16:7

The prophet Samuel was sent by God to anoint the next king of Israel. It wasn't a blind search, and it wasn't a matter of examining applications for the job. God sent Samuel to a specific family. One of the sons of Jesse was to be the new king. But Samuel didn't initially choose the correct son.

> *When they [Jesse and his sons] arrived, Samuel saw Eliab and thought, "Surely the LORD's anointed stands here before the LORD."*
> *But the LORD said to Samuel, "Do not consider his appearance or his height, for I have rejected him. The LORD does not look at the things man looks at. Man looks at the outward appearance, but the LORD looks at the heart."*
> *Then Jesse called Abinadab and had him pass in front of Samuel. But Samuel said, "The LORD has not chosen this one either." Jesse then had Shammah pass by, but Samuel said, "Nor has the LORD chosen this one." Jesse had seven of his sons pass before Samuel, but Samuel said to him, "The LORD has not chosen these." So he asked Jesse, "Are these all the sons you have?"*

"There is still the youngest," Jesse answered, "but he is tending the sheep."

Samuel said, "Send for him; we will not sit down until he arrives."

So he sent and had him brought in. He was ruddy, with a fine appearance and handsome features.

Then the LORD said, "Rise and anoint him; he is the one."

—1 Samuel 16:6–12

Expectations do not have to be based on what is obvious. Just as my elementary students were not typically labeled by most as ladies and gentlemen, David was not the obvious appointee for king. But God knew his capabilities.

Expect the best, not the worst, from your child. But please have realistic expectations, because if they are beyond what is in the realm of possibility, you and your child will both be disappointed.

Impossible Demands

I sat in the yard with a young mother, and we lazily watched her children playing. Before we knew it, her two-year-old had gone beyond the limits of the play area. "Olivia," her mother said, "come over here." When Olivia didn't obey, Mom tied the command to a consequence. "Olivia, you must be back here by the time I count to three or I will have to spank you."

As I calculated the distance between our lawn chairs and Olivia's location and also factored in her ability to cover that ground at top speed, I realized that there was absolutely no way that Olivia could reach us by the count of three. Before Mom could even start to count, I suggested that she reconsider her demand. "I don't think she can possibly do what you have asked her to do. Maybe you should amend your order. You could tell her that by the time you count to three she must be heading back in our direction." Mom agreed. Her expectations had been too high. It was not possible for her daughter to experience success. The expectation, in this case the order, was beyond the realm of possibility. Mom modified her instruction, and Olivia was able to comply.

What about you? Do you have unrealistic expectations for your child? Do you issue impossible demands? When I called my students ladies and gentlemen, I knew they were able to behave as such. And when they failed to do so, I simply reminded them of what I knew they were capable of doing. As you evaluate your expectations for your child, be sure to eliminate expectations that are too low and those that are too high.

Step 1: Aim high, but not beyond the sky. And after you have done that, it is time to . . .

STEP ❷ *Catch your child in the act of doing something right.*

"Therefore encourage one another and build each other up, just as in fact you are doing."
—1 Thessalonians 5:11

I first heard this action step from Wayne Rice, the co-founder of Youth Specialties and founder of Understanding Your Teenager seminars. What is meant by the challenge to "catch your child in the act of doing something right"? Undoubtedly, your child is doing many, many things that are commendable. The truth is that too often, parents fail to notice those things. Instead, they focus on the things done poorly or incorrectly. The Bible verse above is one of my favorites. It is an illustration of Step 2. The writer of 1 Thessalonians waited for the folks he was serving to "do something right." In this case, they were encouraging one another. He was applauding their encouragement. "Keep it up. I like what I see and hear you doing!" That is the implication of the last words of that verse, "just as in fact you are doing." The Thessalonians were being encouraged for their encouragement. They were doing it right!

OF ALL THE FORMS OF DISCIPLINE AND BEHAVIOR MODIFICATION, *REWARDING DESIRABLE BEHAVIOR* WAS RANKED THE MOST EFFECTIVE.

WAY TO GO!

I love you.
How thoughtful.
I know you can do it.
That's a good point.
You're terrific.
You are really improving.
That was a thoughtful thing to do.
That's OK—Nobody's perfect.
I'm proud of you.
You made the right decision.
Good thinking!
Thanks for your help.

Will you forgive me?
I understand.
I love you.[1]

And your child is doing many things right. You have the opportunity to encourage that behavior. Which leads to the next choice in intentional parenting. Step 1: Aim high, but not beyond the sky; Step 2: Catch your child in the act of doing something right. And be sure to . . .

STEP ❸ *Applaud* the product and *the process.*

> *"Brothers, I do not consider myself yet to have taken hold of it. But one thing I do: Forgetting what is behind and straining toward what is ahead, I press on toward the goal to win the prize for which God has called me heavenward in Christ Jesus."*
> —Philippians 3:13–14

All of the A+ spelling papers were on display on the bulletin board. They were the end product of a week's work. The students who spelled each word correctly were being applauded—and rightfully so. It isn't easy to learn how to spell a new set of twenty words in just one week.

I am all for giving accolades to top performers. But what about applauding the ongoing process as well as the end product? If your student is diligent in studying those spelling words each evening—for example, writing them five times apiece—I believe that being conscientious should be rewarded. Almost every student knows that if getting an A+ on the final test is the *only* performance worthy of applause, there is more than one way for her to achieve that goal. If Tommy, who sits just to her right, is a great speller, she could copy Tommy's work and join the group whose test papers are on display. Unfortunately, when *that* performance is applauded, the act of cheating is applauded. Look for opportunities to celebrate the process as well as the product.

PRODUCT	PROCESS
A+ on the spelling test	Writing the spelling words five times each
Making the game-winning basket	Shooting free throws over and over
Good manners in public	Good manners at home
Perfect piano recital	Practicing the scales

When you choose to Be The Parent, you will choose to, Step 1: Aim high, but not beyond the sky; Step 2: Catch your child in the act of doing something right; Step 3: Applaud the product *and* the process; and . . .

STEP ❹ *Encourage your child to encourage others.*

"I thank my God every time I remember you. In all my prayers for all of you, I always pray

with joy because of your partnership in the gospel from the first day until now, being confident of this, that he who began a good work in you will carry it on to completion until the day of Christ Jesus."
—Philippians 1:3–6

I remember seeing a terrific example of this on a high school football field. There was a receiver who had just gone out of the game. His replacement had come in to deliver the play to the quarterback, and the call was for a long pass into the end zone. The quarterback faded back and let go of the ball in a near-perfect spiral, which ended up in the hands of the replacement receiver. He clutched the ball and scampered into the end zone, unscathed. Touchdown! The crowd went wild, and as my eyes tracked the receiver on the sidelines, I realized that he was as excited as those in the hometown stands. He raced out onto the field and was the first to congratulate the other receiver—the receiver who had taken his place, the receiver who would get all the applause for his performance. I wanted to run onto the field myself and congratulate the young man who was the encourager. His unselfish behavior demonstrated character that should be applauded.

Moms and Dads are cheerleaders.
They cheer when their children succeed.
They cheer up their children when they
    don't succeed.
And perhaps more importantly, they cheer
    their children

as their children cheer those who
succeed
and cheer up those who don't succeed.*

*adapted from *It's a Mom Thing* by Kendra Smiley

Brother vs. Brother

A large part of sibling rivalry is the inability to cheer one another on and to applaud one another's successes. But the opposite of sibling rivalry is encouragement.

Jeff and Jerry are brothers. As youngsters, the boys were best friends, playing together and choosing similar activities and interests. By the time I got to know them, however, the friendship was tenuous at best. What happened to cause these siblings to be at odds with one another? I'm sure the answer is more complicated than I can imagine, but I do know one thing about their growing-up years. Their father continually created competition between the brothers. They competed athletically and academically, and the dad was always prepared to proclaim a winner and a loser in the contests. Can you imagine the amount of stress placed on the relationship the brothers had with one another? Sibling rivalry was actually encouraged by their father.

Competition or Congratulations

How sad! That example may be extreme. But how can you encourage your children to *encourage* one another? Obviously, do not structure competition between your children. Rather look for opportunities to congratulate. You can also help each one of your children to identify their natural talents and develop them. Chances are each child will have a different skill that he can improve and enjoy. Even as a youngster, our eldest son loved sports. He especially enjoyed football and is today an assistant coach at a Division 1 school. Our second son managed to turn his fondness for horses into a summer job before he was even fifteen —and eventually into a career as a veterinarian. Our youngest son was helping me "bus" the dinner dishes when he was only two. He innocently threw a glass into the kitchen sink with such force that it shattered into pieces. I encouraged him to be a little gentler in the future, and then for the next sixteen years I watched him play hours and hours of "pitch and catch" with his dad. Today, this left-hander pitches for his Division 1 college team. When the youngest made the university team, his older brothers took partial credit. Did they ever play ball with him? If they did, it wasn't much. But they *did* support him, applaud his successes, and share in the pain of his defeats. They were bonded because of encouragement.

Sibling rivalry is not a requirement. And when you choose to Be The Parent, you can do a great deal to see that it is not a factor in the family dynamics. Instead you can foster sibling rapport and congratulate sibling success. You can choose to encourage and choose to, Step 1: Aim high, but not beyond the sky; Step 2: Catch your child in the act of doing something right; Step 3: Applaud the product *and* the process; Step 4: Encourage your child to encourage others; and finally . . .

STEP ❺ *Teach your child to praise God.*

"I praise you because I am fearfully and wonderfully made."
—Psalm 139:14

Years ago there was a book called *Hurting People Hurt People.* I don't think anyone can argue with that concept. I also believe that *discouraged people discourage people.* One of the best antidotes for discouragement is to praise God. Praising Him shifts the attention from you to the Lord. It has been my experience that the child (or adult for that matter) who is focused on herself finds it very difficult to encourage others or even to be encouraged. After all, it is "all about me." When you teach your child to give praise to God, you are teaching her to take the focus off herself and put it on her heavenly Father.

Praise God

"But thou art holy, O thou that inhabitest the praises of Israel" (Psalm 22:3 KJV). Just think of it, God is as close as the praise of His children. But what if He feels far away? I remember seeing a bumper sticker that read, "If you feel like God is far away, guess who moved."

God inhabits your praises and the praises of your child. He lives there! When a youngster learns to give thanks and praise to God, she is reminded that God is in control. Since "every good and perfect gift is from above," praising God for those gifts is an important habit to instill in your child (James 1:17). Furthermore, an intentional parent models praising God not merely for *what* He does but praising Him for *who* He is. The child who learns to praise God is the child who encourages and is encouraged by God's presence.

> **ACTION STEPS:**
>
> **STEP ❶** Aim high, but not beyond the sky.
>
> **STEP ❷** Catch your child in the act of doing something right.
>
> **STEP ❸** Applaud the product *and* the process.
>
> **STEP ❹** Encourage your child to encourage others.
>
> **STEP ❺** Teach your child to praise God.

A Good Word from John —The Resident Dad

After the death of Moses the servant of the LORD, the LORD said to Joshua son of Nun, Moses' aide: . . . "Be strong and courageous, because you will lead these people to inherit the land I swore to their forefathers to give them. Be strong and courageous. Be careful to obey all the law my servant Moses gave you; do not turn from it to the right or to the left, that you may be successful wherever you go. . . . Have I not commanded you? Be strong and courageous. Do not be terrified; do not be discouraged, for the LORD your God will be with you wherever you go."
—Joshua 1:1, 6–7, 9

A highly successful Division 1 baseball coach was asked the secret to his success. His answer was, to be an encourager! What is it about encouragement that is so powerful? Besides making the recipient feel good, encouragement gives confidence and promotes security. Encouragement moves people toward their best performances and can actually nudge them beyond what they think is possible.

In the roles of parent, teacher, coach, and military officer, I have witnessed firsthand the positive effect that encouragement has on people. I have watched young boys and girls surprise themselves as their performance has exceeded their expectations. And it has been, in no small part, as a result of encouragement.

"You can do it."

"Don't sell yourself short."

"It only takes one."

"You've got what it takes."

These kinds of words spur young and old alike to do their best.

Your child thrives on your encouragement. She wants you to help her see the possibilities that exist. She needs you to believe in her when peers, demeaning adults, or circumstances try to knock her down or hold her back. She desires you to have a positive picture of her potential.

As we see from the verses above, God was a wonderful encourager to Joshua. He knew what a difficult job Joshua had and how important it was for him to succeed. The Lord also knew that His words of encouragement would be a powerful influence.

Mom or Dad, be strong and courageous. Your task is not easy.

Mom or Dad, be strong and courageous. Your task will take commitment.

Mom or Dad, be strong and courageous. God's promise to Joshua is God's promise to believers today. "Do not be terrified. Do not be discouraged, for the LORD your God will be with you wherever you go."

Note:
1. Wayne Rice, *Understanding Your Teenager Seminar Notebook* (Lakeside, Calif. 2005), 27.

Choose to Discipline in Love

There is no easy answer when it comes to discipline, no cookie-cutter, one-size-fits-all approach. Thankfully, the Bible provides us with principles that answer many questions about discipline and child rearing. Discipline is an important biblical fundamental. It is the loving thing to do, and it *does* work. Let's take a look at some of the things that can distract a parent from administering loving discipline.

My Normal

In my home growing up, my mother was solely responsible for discipline. My father was forty-five years old when I was born and referred to me as his "built-in grandchild." That is also the way he related to me. He was there to spoil me but not to give structure and guidance. My mother, on the other hand, was younger and much more diligent with discipline. She set the rules and enforced the consequences. Although I was not a strong-willed child, I was still relatively spunky. Much of my time was spent trying to discover new and creative ways to avoid following the rules and avoid receiving discipline. I was very successful ... for a while. Unfortunately, those "successes" didn't help much after I became an adult.

His Normal

My husband's growing-up experience was different from mine. His father was a strong disciplinarian, and there was no room for creative disobedience. I have already pointed out that the definition of *normal* is whatever happened in your family of origin, no matter how bizarre it might have been. When John and I were married, he brought his normal into our family, and I brought mine. The challenge was now to establish a new normal for our family.

The very fact that two families are being combined can be the source of many problems in disciplining your child.

"You're being too tough on him!" is the contention of one parent.

"You never make the consequences adequate. She is getting away with murder!" is the claim of the other parent.

When their child realizes the discrepancy, it is likely he will capitalize on it and pit one parent against the other. This leads to the all-important first step for Mom and Dad:

STEP ❶ *Sing off the same song sheet.*

"May the God who gives endurance and encouragement give you a spirit of unity among yourselves as you follow Christ Jesus."
—Romans 15:5

I realize that some of you reading this book may be single parents. That means that the daily "song sheet" is selected entirely by you. As you receive help in your parenting from your parents or from friends, it is important that all the adults sing from your sheet. It is also ideal if a child's birth parents, though separated or divorced, can come to some degree of harmony as they attempt to help their child mature.

The idea of being in agreement when it comes to discipline may seem elementary, but it is not achieved by the majority of couples. This can be a big distraction. What can you do if you and your spouse do not see eye to eye?

First of all, you must dialogue with one another and determine where each of you stands on discipline. It is very helpful if you cannot only state the definition of effective discipline in your opinion but can also identify *why* you have chosen your position. At a recent Be the Parent conference, a woman told us that her husband had announced that she

SOMETHING TO TALK ABOUT: 64% OF CHRISTIAN PARENTS ADMIT THEY SOMETIMES DISAGREE WITH THE OTHER PARENT ABOUT DISCIPLINE. DON'T GIVE UP— NEGOTIATE AND PRAY TOWARD UNITY!

was to be completely responsible for disciplining their children. She went on to share that this responsibility was overwhelming her. My question to her was, "Why? Why did your husband give you the entire responsibility?" After a moment or two of thought, she concluded that perhaps it was because he was raised by a violent, abusive father and had unhealed emotional scars from his childhood. That was probably a pretty accurate analysis. There is always a reason why people function or feel the way they do about discipline. If you cannot put your finger on it, or if what is transpiring doesn't make sense, it is probably because you don't have enough information. So gather more information and talk with one another about it.

Compromise

If you and your spouse are not in agreement about how to discipline your child, it is time to compromise. Now is not the time to be unbending. Find the middle ground of discipline that both of you can support. It doesn't actually have to be in the middle. If you are certain that you have taken the better position, be prepared to defend that position and present persuasive arguments so that the compromise will be adequate.

Parents, it is extremely important that you are in one accord about how and when you will discipline your child. As you choose to Be The Parent, you must be diligent to, Step 1: Sing off the same song sheet. And as that song sheet is agreed upon, be sure to . . .

STEP ❷ *Follow the basics of discipline.*

"Do not withhold discipline from a child."
—Proverbs 23:13

No Anger

Probably the most fundamental rule is to never discipline in anger. We hear a great deal about abuse these days and want to completely avoid behavior that might be classified as such. Most people think of physical punishment when they hear the word *abuse*. In reality, screaming, shrieking, using demeaning words, ignoring, or neglecting a child can all be forms of abuse.

How do you avoid this inappropriate, ineffective behavior as a parent? The all-important first step is to realize that the risk of abuse exists when discipline is administered in anger. Being aware of this fact and alert to the possibility of becoming angry will help you keep your temper in check.

And Breathe Deeply . . .

When our first child was on the way, John and I took Lamaze birthing classes at the area hospital. In those classes we discovered the importance of the cleansing breath—a deep, full and controlled inhaling, followed by a slow and controlled exhaling. I'm not sure of all the benefits of this maneuver, but I do know it had a calming effect on me (something I recall being in need of during childbirth)! Lamaze breathing has served me well, not just during the births of my three sons but throughout the years. In fact, on more than one occasion, I have taken a Lamaze cleansing breath prior to administering discipline in order to help me *respond* to the misbehavior of my child and not *react* to it. In fact, taking a cleansing breath is actually something I advocate. The simple, calming action of taking a deep breath can help a parent regain composure and can eliminate the instantaneous reaction of anger. A Lamaze cleansing breath, used by Mom or Dad, is akin to pausing and counting silently to ten. Either action helps establish focus and eliminate anger when punishment is delivered.

No Emotion

Although I was typically successful at disciplining our children without anger, I later learned that I still had room for improvement. Aaron, our middle son, and I coauthored the book *Aaron's Way: The Journey of a Strong-Willed Child.* As a former strong-willed child turned responsible adult, Aaron agreed that disciplining in anger was counterproductive, but he went on to expand on that idea.

> Mom's suggestion that discipline ought to never be administered in anger is a good one. But I want you to think about a more radical possibility. . . . What if an attempt was made to discipline with no emotion whatsoever? We all know it is wrong to discipline in anger. I'm suggesting that neither disciplining in sympathy nor frustration nor pity nor commiseration is the optimal condition.
> . . . That doesn't indicate lack of love or caring; it is merely healthy detachment in delivering punishment.

Emotional discipline seems to be a trap that mothers fall into more often than fathers. A child can actually choose to elicit emotion from you by pushing all your buttons. This behavior acts to trap you in an emotional corner so that you will avoid administering discipline the next time. (Never forget how bright your child is!) Think about the last time you had to administer discipline. Did you do it without emotion?

THE BASICS OF DISCIPLINE

- No anger.
- No emotion.
- Pick your battles wisely.
- Win those battles.
- Set legitimate consequences.

Pick 'em and Win

That leads to the next basic: Pick your battles wisely. And those you pick, you must win. Because of the second part of this basic rule of discipline, it is obvious that you do not want to pick a multitude of battles. Let's return to a family we met in an earlier chapter. Let's go back to the dad and his daughter in the pizza place. The dad told his daughter to stay in her chair after she was finished eating because several adults in their party were not finished. As soon as the words left his lips, she hopped down from her chair and went around the table to visit with folks on the other side. He initially chose to fight the stay-in-your-chair battle. But he did not win. The act of walking around to the other side of the table became a bad thing because she was specifically told to stay in her chair.

Crying Wolf

"Do this!" you say. There is no response from your child and no consequence from you. "Do that!" you command. And again there is no compliance and no follow-up. You are crying wolf. If you choose battles to fight and do not administer the consequences when your orders are defied, it doesn't take long for your words to be ignored. Sadly, this will become routine and your words will be ignored the time you really do mean business, when there really *is* a wolf!

ON AVERAGE, CHRISTIAN PARENTS RANKED THE FORMS OF DISCIPLINE METHODS OF *SPANKING, VERBAL REPRIMANDS, TIME-OUTS,* AND *ASSIGNMENT OF WORK* AT SIMILAR LEVELS OF EFFECTIVENESS. *REWARDING DESIRABLE BEHAVIOR* AND *TAKING AWAY PRIVILEGES* RANKED HIGHER.

Mom or Dad, think before you speak! Don't make demands that you don't intend to enforce. Don't choose to fight so many battles that your child cannot possibly comply with every instruction. Don't burden yourself with a plethora of rules and subsequent penalties you must impose. If you are issuing a vast quantity of rules, the odds increase for noncompliance and inadequate follow-up.

Legitimate Consequences

To win the battles you choose to fight you must set legitimate consequences. Legitimate consequences are logical and fitting parental responses to misbehavior. There are many forms of discipline available to you as a parent. The ones you choose will depend, in part, upon the nature of your child and her age. This is where, again, you need to know your child (and the situation) to determine the appropriate method of discipline. For some children, time-outs are effective. Restricting privileges is also a form of discipline that can modify behavior. And, of course, we do not want to forget the ever controversial . . . *spanking.*

Spare the Rod

"He who spares the rod hates his son, but he who loves him is careful to discipline him."
—Proverbs 13:24

When our children were young, we visited a childhood friend of mine one evening for dinner. This couple also had three children and a live-in nanny. The adults ate dinner in the formal dining room and the six children and the nanny ate in the kitchen. When we drove away from their home, our children asked us many questions about this new discovery, this nanny.

"Why do they have a nanny?" one son asked.

"To take care of Cameron, their youngest son," I replied.

"Well, she's not doing a very good job. He didn't behave at dinner." All the boys agreed on this one and one of our children continued the questioning.

"Is a nanny expensive?"

"I'm not sure what it costs to have a nanny," I answered.

"Wouldn't it be a lot cheaper if they just had a paddle?"

I had to laugh. "Wouldn't it be cheaper?" Yes, I suppose it would be. Just have a paddle, the source of discipline that was familiar to our children. No nanny necessary!

As I sit at my computer and write, nanny shows are all the rage on television. These shows have many good points when it comes to discipline but fail to reveal the complete truth about spanking. God's Word specifically endorses spanking as a form of discipline. So do many experts.

> Children are so tremendously variable that it is sometimes hard to believe that they are all members of the same human family. You can crush some children with nothing more than a stern look; others seem to require strong and even painful disciplinary measures to make a vivid impression.[1]

There are specific guiding principles that can help you use spanking as an effective and appropriate form of loving discipline.

1. A spanking is serious business. It is not to be used indiscriminately as a punishment or consequence for every misdemeanor.

2. A spanking should be done with a paddle and not with your hand, separating the implement of discipline from the loving parent who has administered the discipline.

3. A spanking should be applied to the child's bottom where there is plenty of padding.

4. A spanking should be of sufficient force to deter the repetition of the undesired behavior. If you don't know how much force to employ, you can try the paddle on your own thigh. That will give you a gauge of the strength you need to use.

As a child, my temperament was such that my mother's threat to "get the yardstick" was sufficient to dissuade me from continuing the negative behavior. To many children, threats mean nothing, especially if the threats have been idle ones up to this point.

Show me what you've got! Give me your best shot! Those thoughts go through the minds of many defiant children, though they are too smart to actually utter those words. Adequate, loving discipline will probably bring rapid results. But don't be discouraged if your discipline does not immediately change your child's behavior. If you are certain that you are administering sufficient punishment and there is no abrupt change in his behavior, he may simply be testing to see if your follow-through was a onetime fluke. If the discipline caused your child to hesitate and at least contemplate his bad behavior, you're moving in the right direction. Be encouraged!

Uncomfortable

There comes a time of physical maturity for your child when neither time-outs nor spankings are legitimate options for discipline. Many parents morph time-outs into being "grounded." It is important that you think through the ramifications of any chosen discipline. When you ground your child, for example, you are also grounded.

As far as spanking an older child, it is demeaning to spank a child who has entered puberty. Because the time of this transition to adulthood varies from child to child, it is my recommendation that you stop spanking at the first indication that your child is near puberty. The fact that this form of discipline is no longer appropriate does not mean there are no consequences for defiance. It is still necessary for you to make your child uncomfortable. How do you know what will make your child uncomfortable? You must know your child. What are his likes and dislikes? What things occupy his leisure time? What are the hot topics he brings up for discussion? How would he spend a gift of money if he had no input or guidance from you? The answers to these questions help define his interests. They also give you insight into what will motivate him.

If there is more than one child in your family, there is more than one strategy of discipline that will be effective in your family. A very tenderhearted child may respond to a heart-to-heart conversation where you express your dismay at his poor behavior. Another child may respond better to the restriction of privileges. If your child is a video game whiz, you can limit his playing time. Our eldest enjoyed television, especially sports on TV. Pulling the plug was a very effective way to discipline him.

Mother Knows Best

A woman I know, a single mom, was a diligent student of her daughters. She knew them well and knew their likes and dislikes. At one point her younger daughter decided to defy the rules of their home. Mom was well aware that this daughter highly valued her privacy. After being warned and choosing to disobey, the teenager came home to find that the door to her bedroom had been removed— precisely what her mother had told her the consequence would be. There were no men in the house. There was a single mom and two daughters. Mom didn't make this choice to embarrass her daughter; removing the door was a consequence that made her daughter uncomfortable. And it wasn't long before this young lady changed her behavior and earned back her bedroom door. What legitimate consequence will make your child uncomfortable? These things are all basics of discipline.

An intentional parent chooses to, Step 1: Sing off the same song sheet; Step 2: Follow the basics of discipline; and . . .

STEP ❸ *Think long-term.*

> *"For I know the plans I have for you,"* declares the LORD, *"plans to prosper you and not to harm you, plans to give you hope and a future."*
> —Jeremiah 29:11

The Scripture verse above tells us that God has plans for us. He is thinking long-term. That isn't always easy for a parent to do. The current, the urgent, and the here and now all seem to shout so loudly that many times a parent cannot hear the still, small, faraway voice of the future. This can be a distraction to loving discipline.

"I told Joshua he would have to pick up his toys before we left for the T-ball game or he would not be allowed to play T-ball that afternoon," a mother told me one day. "He had plenty of time to get the job done."

Time went by and Joshua did not pick up his toys as

instructed by his mother. She reminded him again and again as the clock ticked away the minutes. Finally it was time to go, and the toys were still scattered around the room. We already know from the stated consequences that Joshua would not be playing T-ball that afternoon, right? Hang on and listen to what Mom told me next.

"I realized that Joshua had not done what I asked him to do. But I knew he really enjoyed playing T-ball and it was the last week, so I told him he could go to T-ball and pick up his toys after the game," she explained.

Poor Joshua. He won the battle and did not pick up his toys before T-ball. Poor Mom. She got confused. For just a minute, she thought she was raising a T-ball player. She was shortsighted. She forgot that her job, her long-term goal, was to raise a young man with integrity who understood and respected discipline. I can imagine Joshua thinking, "Who wants to go to T-ball? Not me. Some of those kids don't even run the bases in the right direction. She'll probably let me go anyway. It's really my mom who likes T-ball. I'm not picking up my toys."

A parent choosing loving discipline will make every effort to, Step 1: Sing off the same song sheet; Step 2: Follow the basics of discipline; Step 3: Think long-term; and . . .

STEP ❹ *Be consistent.*

> *"So be careful to do what the LORD your God has commanded you; do not turn aside to the right or to the left."*
> —Deuteronomy 5:32

Your child depends on the assurance of your consistency. He wants to know that the rules you set and the consequences you have established will be fair and will not change on a whim. Your consistent, fair discipline will foster his security. Let's examine fair discipline for just a moment. That is a concept that baffles many parents.

Fair discipline means that the punishment fits the crime and can even mean determining the distinction of crime versus carelessness. Spilling juice is not an act of disobedience; it is childish carelessness. Punishing a child because he accidentally spilled his orange juice is not fitting. Instead, it is appropriate to ask him in a calm voice to try to be more careful or to be sure his glass is not near the edge of the table, and then have him help you clean up the juice.

When you tell your child not to go into the street, and he chooses to leave the sidewalk and venture into the street, this is disobedience. (And is also very dangerous.) He has defied your order and must receive an appropriate, uncomfortable consequence in order to keep him from repeating the disobedience.

Whenever possible, children need to know the consequences for their disobedience before they disobey. They want you to be consistent. If the little boy who ran into the street knew he would be spanked and the spanking made him uncomfortable, chances are he would stay on the sidewalk in the future. In most cases, it is not fair to announce the punishment after the offense. If the child realizes *after* his poor choice that he is going to receive discipline, he has been robbed of his ability to make a good choice and avoid the punishment. If this was the first time the little boy had entered the street, a stern reprimand indicating that any further infractions of the rule would result in a spanking is completely appropriate. And then, if the little boy chose to disobey, the consequence must be administered.

Be sure your child is paying attention to you when you make him aware of what will happen as the result of choosing to break a specific rule. In order to know that your child is listening, you can have him repeat the instruction and the consequence for disobedience. Being sure your child understands the instruction and the consequence leaves the decision in that child's hands. If he chooses to disobey, he has chosen the consequence. The child knows what is expected and what will happen if a punishment is necessary. The decision about whether or not to disobey and accept the discipline is totally his. You are simply the one administering the consequence your child has chosen.

Yes and No

"Let your 'Yes' be 'Yes' and your 'No' be 'No.'"
—Matthew 5:37

"Dad, may I go to the park with Jason?"

"No!"

"Please, Dad. We're only going to be gone for an hour because Jason has to go to piano lessons."

"No!"

"There's a new slide and it is terrific . . . really tall and curly!"

"OK. Be back in an hour."

What is wrong with the dialogue above? Dad's answer was no . . . not just once, but more than once. But this repetition didn't stop his son's demands. He knew better. He knew that Dad's no didn't really mean no. It meant "Maybe. Give me more information." It meant "I'm tired. I just got home from work, and I don't want to think about anything for a few minutes." It meant "I always say no first, but I usually change my mind."

This dad's no was something that could be debated. And that was precisely what his son did. Dad was not consistent. If you do not want to debate and negotiate each time you reply to a request from your child, be sure you legitimately consider the request before you respond.

Radical Yes

I have known parents who think it is their duty to answer no to the majority of the requests made by their child. I support and encourage you as a parent to answer yes whenever possible. What if you took the time to consider the request your child was making and then said yes as often as you could? I am not suggesting that you allow your child to do dangerous, destructive, or outlandish things. I am simply suggesting that if you start today to really listen to what your child is asking, you will probably realize that you can usually give permission to his request.

Here's an idea. For the next twenty-four hours, commit to being a member of the radical yes group. Listen to your child's request, evaluate it, and say yes if at all possible. There is a very logical reason for this strategy. Saying yes whenever possible gives more weight to your answer of no. When you take the time to evaluate the request your child is making and to actually respond to it instead of react, your child will be more discriminating in his appeals, and you will spend less time in debate. If you always say no initially, your child will be more apt to keep on arguing and questioning your decision. Give the radical yes group a try. It might prove worthy of a lifetime membership.

When you choose to Be The Parent, you choose to, Step 1: Sing off the same song sheet; Step 2: Follow the basics of discipline; Step 3: Think long-term; Step 4: Be consistent; and finally . . .

STEP ❺ *Reject the parenting lies.*

> *"I have told you these things, so that in me you may have peace. In this world you will have trouble. But take heart! I have overcome the world."*
> —John 16:33

Christ has overcome the world, but the world is still clamoring to have its lies and half-truths about parenting accepted and believed.

THE LIES OF THE WORLD

Your child *will* be difficult.
You *will* experience the terrible twos and the turbulent teens.
Your child *will* rebel.
All teenagers lie and drink and have sex.
All children disrespect authority.
You *ARE NOT* equipped to be the parent.

THE TRUTH OF THE WORD

> *"From the lips of children and infants you have ordained praise."*
> —Psalm 8:2

"A wise son brings joy to his father."
—Proverbs 10:1

"The father of a righteous man has great joy; he who has a wise son delights in him."
—Proverbs 23:24

"A man who loves wisdom brings joy to his father."
—Proverbs 29:3

"Her children arise and call her blessed."
—Proverbs 31:28

The lies of the world are a distraction to loving discipline. A parent who chooses to discipline in love does not passively accept these lies as the truth but instead becomes familiar with the truth of the Word of God. This is as simple as taking a daily dose of Proverbs.

One-a-Day Proverbs

The book of Proverbs in the Old Testament is made up of thirty-one chapters. Most of the months of the year have thirty-one days. (Do you see where I'm going?) On the first day of the month, the dosage is Proverbs 1. On the second day of the month, it's Proverbs 2. It is easy to remember your daily

WHOSE OPINION MATTERS THE MOST? CHRISTIAN MOMS AND DADS ADMIT THAT THEIR PARENTING SKILLS ARE MORE LIKELY INFLUENCED BY *THEIR* MOTHERS THAN THE BIBLE.

dose. Don't worry if you miss a day. Take part in one-a-day Proverbs for five or six months, and you will read each chapter multiple times. In order to supplement your daily dosage, I suggest you have a pen and paper in hand when you read so you can journal. Jot down the specific verses for the day that address parenting. You will be amazed what you will discover and your journal will fill up with the truth—the whole truth and nothing but the truth—the Word of God!

ACTION STEPS:

STEP ❶ Sing off the same song sheet.

STEP ❷ Follow the basics of discipline.

STEP ❸ Think long-term.

STEP ❹ Be consistent.

STEP ❺ Reject the parenting lies.

A Good Word from John —The Resident Dad

Are you ready for a sad story? Read on:

> *And the LORD said to Samuel: "See, I am about to do something in Israel that will make the ears of everyone who hears of it tingle. At that time I will carry out against Eli everything I spoke against his family—from beginning to*

end. For I told him that I would judge his fam-
ily forever because of the sin he knew about; his
sons made themselves contemptible, and he
failed to restrain them."
—1 Samuel 3:11–13

Eli knew his sons were making poor decisions and he "failed to restrain them." God knew about the bad decisions too. In response to Eli's lack of discipline of his sons, God didn't say, "Oh, that's all right, Eli; boys will be boys." God didn't say, "That's all right, Eli; all teenagers go through times of rebellion." God didn't say, "Don't worry about how your kids have been behaving; you've been busy at work." God didn't say, "You did the best you could, Eli. That's good enough." No, God said, "Eli, you knew about the sin of your sons, and you failed to restrain them."

Your responsibility is to Be The Parent, and a big part of that is restraining or disciplining your child—in partnership, following the basics, thinking long-term, being consistent, and rejecting the lies of the world. No parent wants to hear the words that Eli heard from God.

We live in a time when many things undermine the confidence of parents and dissuade them from seeking and applying biblical truth. It is difficult to parent when a professional tells you, in opposition to Scripture, that spanking administered as loving discipline will cause your child to hit others. It is difficult to discipline effectively when your child threatens to call 911 if you put him in a time-out. It is difficult to Be The Parent when television gives the impression *that the child should be in control or when you and your spouse don't agree on a course of action.*

It is difficult, but there are no excuses. Your responsibility is to seek the truth and then to confidently discipline your child in love.

Note:
1. Dr. James Dobson, *Dare to Discipline* (Wheaton: Tyndale, 1986), 44.

Choose to Allow Failure and Success

I remember when our eldest son celebrated his eleventh birthday, and his grandmother gave him a crisp, new twenty-dollar bill. This gift was a real treat and something he could spend any way he chose. I took him to the mall to exchange that twenty-dollar bill for something special. Spending his birthday money was our only goal, so the toy store was our destination. When we arrived he immediately headed for the electronics section and immersed himself in studying the various games. He looked at the graphics on each box and read every word of the descriptions, contemplating his various options. Unlike today, twenty dollars would buy a new computer game or a handheld electronic device. Matthew wanted to be certain that he selected the very best one. Methodically, he studied each toy in the price range and finally, after much deliberation, decided upon a specific one.

With the birthday selection in his hand, he made his way to the checkout counter. There were two or three customers ahead of him in line, so Matthew would have to wait for a little while longer to enjoy his gift. As he stood there, the impulse items on the long counter caught his eye. Matthew picked up one or two of them and quickly glanced at the claims on the back of the boxes. When he finally reached his destination, I was shocked to hear him say, "I changed my mind. I want this instead."

He showed me the alternative, the shiny impulse item, chosen on a whim. "Are you sure?" I asked. He nodded, and I said nothing more.

Matthew paid for the new toy, and we headed for the parking lot. Mission accomplished, or so I thought. He immediately tore open the package and began to fiddle with his birthday purchase. We buckled up and I started the car. Literally, before we got out of the parking lot of the Tippecanoe Mall in Lafayette, Indiana, he reached into the front seat and handed me the newly acquired item. "Take this, Mom, and throw it away. It's junk and just seeing it makes me feel bad." I can still hear his words to this day.

Feeling Bad

He was not the only one who felt bad that day. After hearing the disappointment in his voice, I wasn't sure which one of us felt worse. I took the toy and disposed of it. "That's OK, Matthew," I said. "Grandma will probably give you twenty dollars again next year."

That's what I said. But that is not what I *wanted* to

say. I wanted to say, "Here's twenty dollars. Let's go back in and get something else. Now this time, try to make a better choice." I didn't want my son to feel bad. I didn't want to feel bad. I wanted to rescue him from the poor choice he had just made. The truth of the matter is, that day I didn't have an extra twenty to give to him. And in retrospect, I am happy that the money wasn't available. Through the grace of God, I didn't rescue him. That is the first and often the most difficult step.

STEP ❶ *Resist the rescue.*

> *"The LORD is slow to anger, abounding in love and forgiving sin and rebellion. Yet he does not leave the guilty unpunished."*
> —Numbers 14:18

Life is full of consequences for decisions. Good consequences follow good decisions and bad consequences follow bad decisions. The Word of God as quoted above talks specifically about the consequences for sin. As parents, it is important that we allow our children to experience the consequences for a poor choice. Resist the rescue.

66% OF CHRISTIAN PARENTS ADMIT THAT THEY SOMETIMES SHELTER THEIR CHILD FROM EXPERIENCING FAILURE.

No Lunch

Most parents have brought an occasional lunch or band instrument to school for their forgetful son or daughter. Is that a rescue? In a sense it is, but the key is to (1) see to it that your child learns that she is the one who must be responsible, and (2) see to it that your "helpful behavior" is not repeated over and over. It is important to avoid being a parent who is obsessive or irrational. Resist the rescue.

Do not mimic the behavior of one mother I met. Her son didn't seem to be able to remember his sack lunch for school. He forgot it on Monday, and on Tuesday, and on Wednesday, and on Thursday, and on Friday! Hard to believe, isn't it? But it really didn't matter because Joel's mom brought the missing lunch to him day after day after day. This drama actually gets more amazing when you learn that Mom's work location made for a thirty-mile round-trip for the daily lunch delivery. Joel obviously didn't learn and change his behavior because Mom was there to rescue him. Joel didn't take responsibility for remembering his lunch, and Mom didn't encourage him in that pursuit.

Young people like Joel, who are repeatedly rescued, not only become dependent but also do not enjoy their good choices. Fast-forward a few years. When Joel was a little older, he won a fiction writing contest. Rather than enjoying this success, he imagined that his mom knew the judge and had somehow influenced the outcome. Joel had lost his sense of responsibility *and* had been robbed of his freedom to enjoy success. It is a double-edged sword and leads to the next step for intentional parenting. Step 1: Resist the rescue; and . . .

STEP ❷ *Give the freedom to succeed.*

"Choose for yourselves this day whom you will serve."
—Joshua 24:15

Another portion of Joshua 24:15 is quoted more often. We see it on plaques and many have memorized its words. "But as for me and my household, we will serve the LORD." Obviously those are powerful words of encouragement, but I personally find even more challenge in the first part of that verse, the portion quoted above. The first three words alone are empowering. "Choose for yourselves." If you choose to Be The Parent, you will allow your child to fail and succeed.

Nothing to Wear

Long after the twenty-dollar shopping failure, my son Matthew had his first *real* summer job. For years he had helped around the farm, but this particular year, he had interviewed and been hired to work for an accounting office. About two days before he was to begin work, it dawned on him that his current wardrobe was inadequate for office work. I agreed and sent him to the mall with my credit card. I'm not sure when reality sunk in, but at some point I realized what I had done. My son was at the mall with my credit card and with no prior instructions as to what he should purchase or how much he should spend. When I recovered somewhat from my horror, I decided to just wait and see what transpired. About two hours later, my son returned home with multiple bags. As I sat down and braced myself for the fashion show, he opened the first bag. Out came a pair of navy blue dress pants accompanied with this narrative: "These cost five dollars. They are only a size too big, and I can wear a belt." (And actually, they looked very good!) With those words, I relaxed considerably, and when the final item went on display, I had calculated that

Matthew had spent about sixty dollars. Not bad, not bad at all.

I believe that Matthew's ability to outfit himself in office clothes for the summer and spend no more than sixty dollars was aided by the fact that he had not been rescued so many years ago as he foolishly spent his birthday money. He was reaping the benefit of the negative consequences . . . and so was I, as the one paying the credit card bill.

It is not easy as the parent to follow the first steps of resisting the urge to rescue and giving the freedom to succeed, but they are necessary steps in raising confident, responsible adults. The choices in the examples above, shopping with birthday money, remembering or not remembering to bring a lunch, and buying office clothes, were all choices that these kids were capable of making. They were maturity-appropriate.

And that is the next step in our progression. Step 1: Resist the rescue; Step 2: Give the freedom to succeed; and . . .

STEP ❸ *Encourage maturity-appropriate choices.*

"And Jesus grew in wisdom and stature, and in favor with God and men."
—Luke 2:52

Just like your son or daughter, Jesus began as a tiny little baby. And hopefully just like Jesus, your child will change and mature as the verse above states. With the changes in age and maturity, come changes in the choices that are appropriate for your child to make.

You start the parenting job with around-the-clock

demands. Your task is to make every decision for and about this little bundle of joy that was plunked into your lap. You are beyond *necessary;* you are absolutely *vital* to the survival of your child. He or she is not capable of making one choice. This little baby cannot succeed or fail . . . yet.

Before too long, the dependent infant will grow and mature. He is now developing a personality and the desire to make choices. "Do you want some Cheerios? . . . Would you like a drink of juice?" These are simple choices, yet they are choices all the same. And these are just the beginning. Before long your child will choose her favorite color and who she would like to sit by in Sunday school. Eventually, your kids will decide what they will wear, what games they will play, and what videos or television shows they will watch . . . within reason, that is.

They may have a say in some areas but not be fully sanctioned for the final decision. You will decide what choices are appropriate and when they can have the final say.

ON THE RIGHT TRACK: WHILE 69% OF CHRISTIAN PARENTS SAY TELEVISION HAS *SOME* INFLUENCE OVER THE VALUES OF THEIR CHILD, ONLY 19% SAY TELEVISION HAS *A LOT* OF INFLUENCE ON VALUES.

When my eldest, Matthew, was in fifth or sixth grade, I was bound and determined to help him establish a friendship with a certain young man who was close to his age. Why? Because I liked this other boy's mother! I knew that if the two boys became friends, I would have more opportunities to spend time with *my* friend. With great enthusiasm I repeatedly suggested things the boys could do together. My son always seemed hesitant, but I managed to ignore his reticence. Finally, after more than enough suggestions, Matthew simply said, "Mom, you don't *want* me to be friends with him!" That was it. No more. Obviously he knew something I didn't know. I stopped pushing the relationship between the boys and simply enjoyed my occasional interaction with the other child's mother. Before long, I understood the words of my son. He was absolutely right. His age-appropriate decision was a good one, and better than his mom would have made!

The List

I wish I could give you a comprehensive list of when and what your child should be allowed to choose. I cannot. What I can do is encourage you to make those decisions based on biblical absolutes and your own parental preferences. Do not let your child pressure you, guilt you, or shame you into allowing her to make choices that you know she is not mature enough to make. And it doesn't matter what everyone else is doing.

If you allow a choice and then realize that your child is not capable of making a good decision yet in that area, do not dismay. Simply withdraw the privilege until your child has adequately matured. Then try again. For example, you allow your child to play in the unfenced portion of your yard with the instruction not to leave the yard. Later, you discover that she has wandered next door. You withdraw the privilege and limit your child's play area to the fenced-in yard. When you decide that your child is ready to try again, you give her the opportunity.

The children in your family will not all reach levels of maturity at the same time or even at the same age. Be aware of this. They must prove to you they can handle the choices they are allowed to make—and handle them by making good decisions.

My Choice

You will make many determinations, but please do not make any and every decision for your child. Children learn by doing and if you are constantly in control, you are stifling their learning and hurting your relationship with your child.

One of the risks we run into as parents is to fail to realize that our children are constantly changing. They are gaining maturity and experience, and we must adjust in our response to them. It is easy to treat a child as though she is less mature than she actually is. Perhaps as parents we aren't ready for the independence our child has earned. We enjoy her dependence and fail to modify our behavior to fit the changes that have occurred. Remember that your child is maturing physically, mentally, socially, and emotionally, and that this is a good thing.

On one specific occasion John cautioned me to step back and look at how I was treating one of our sons. I was not encouraging him to make maturity-appropriate choices. I had failed to respond to the level of maturity he had attained. When I realized my inappropriate behavior, I changed that behavior, and amazingly our son responded and returned to his relatively delightful self.

Mom or Dad, ask yourself these questions: Have I been encouraging my child to make maturity-appropriate choices? Or have I failed to notice and adjust to the physical, emotional, mental, and social changes that have occurred in his or her life? After your honest evaluation, compare notes with your spouse and give one another feedback. Are both of you allowing those healthy choices? If not, why not? And why not start today? Remember to, Step 1: Resist the rescue; Step 2: Give the freedom to succeed; Step 3: Encourage maturity-appropriate choices; and . . .

STEP ❹ *Continually expand the boundaries.*

"When I was a child, I talked like a child, I thought like a child, I reasoned like a child. When I became a man, I put childish ways behind me."
—1 Corinthians 13:11

Parenthood. Is there any other labor (pun intended) where success is marked by no longer being necessary? As the mother of three grown sons, I make very few choices for them. They are at the ages and stages where the great majority of their choices are made independently, at least independent of me. My role is that of consultant. When one of our sons determines that I *might* have a good idea or some specific knowledge in a particular area, he is quick to ask for help or an opinion. I no longer give a great deal of unsolicited guidance. (Well, OK, on occasion I offer up a few helpful hints, but I try to be conscious of whether or not they have been solicited.) Our adult children are independent. This independence was one of the goals John and I set shortly after they were born. Most parents desire that their children are capable and willing to become mature, responsible, functioning adults. As much as I enjoyed being a "Mommy," I remember the day I realized that

"Mom" was no longer my job description but was instead a term of endearment. And the transition was just that—a transition, an evolution, a gradual change.

Instant Adult

Many parents today think there is something magic about their children reaching eighteen years of age. The truth is, if your child is not making good choices at three years of age or nine or fourteen, there is no magic that will be performed at eighteen years of age. Maturity is a process. And part of that process involves your willingness to gradually and continually enlarge the territory of your child's choices. When this is done from an early age, you will be there to monitor progress and to offer guidance as her territory expands. You will be there to encourage and to teach.

If the world of a baby is the arms of her parents and her crib, the world of a toddler is her home. The older child plays in a fenced-in yard, without the need for constant supervision. And as maturity develops, her world expands to include the neighborhood. A teenager's driver's license offers a great deal of freedom and expanded territory. Finally, your child will probably leave your home and create her own boundaries. You are no longer the one determining the boundaries. But that is OK, because as an intentional parent, one allowing failure and success, you have been training your child for this responsibility and personally preparing for this separation.

When you choose to allow failure and success, you will, Step 1: Resist the rescue; Step 2: Give the freedom to succeed; Step 3: Encourage maturity-appropriate choices; Step 4: Continually expand the boundaries; and . . .

STEP ❺ *Eliminate the vote.*

> *"Let the wise listen and add to their learning,*
> *and let the discerning get guidance."*
> —Proverbs 1:5

It is important to listen to the members of your family and to treat one another with respect. In fact, modeling listening and respect will typically mean that your child will become a listener and be respectful to you. One mistake that is made in the name of respect is to give an equal vote to all members of the family. "Where should we go on vacation? One, two, three votes for the exotic cruise we can't afford. And, yes, I'm voting with you, dear, two votes for camping at the lake. Well, I guess the kids win the vote." Yikes! You may seek the input of every member of the family, but no vote should be taken.

No Democracy

So what does it look like to solicit input but not votes? Let's take that family vacation as an example. I'm guessing your kids are as interesting as mine were. It's always fun to discover how a child defines a perfect vacation. Have you ever asked that question? I'm not suggesting that you insinuate that her suggestion will determine your next summer trip; I'm encouraging you to listen as your child gives you valuable information about her likes and dislikes and dreams. When my children were younger and we talked about possible vacation ideas, I didn't word the questions to suggest we were voting on the destination. First, John and I decided on location and budget. Then I told the kids the things I knew about the location—if there was a water park nearby, if fishing, swimming, or beach play were options, and what attractions were found en route to the destination. With this information in hand, I encouraged each child to tell me what sounded like fun. We usually did this exercise as a family because then we could build and expand on one another's ideas.

There are many things that can be accomplished by soliciting input from your children. First of all, they realize that you are interested in their ideas. I have learned a great deal about my children by listening to their thoughts and opinions. In addition, your children will realize they are capable of formulating an opinion and articulating that opinion. The kids also learn that the more realistic their suggestions, the more likely these are to be implemented. Additionally, I found it entertaining to see that many times the suggestion of a sibling became the "best time of all" for his brother. In our family we combined the educational with the adventurous and the elegant with the offbeat. We also managed to visit church services when we were away from home on Sundays.

Mom or Dad, feel free—in fact feel encouraged—to ask your child for input. But avoid the temptation to let that input become an equal vote.

ACTION STEPS:

STEP ❶ Resist the rescue.

STEP ❷ Give the freedom to succeed.

STEP ❸ Encourage maturity-appropriate choices

STEP ❹ Continually expand the boundaries.

STEP ❺ Eliminate the vote.

A Good Word from John —The Resident Dad

I recently sat on a bench in a local park and watched as children and their parents interacted. The playground equipment in that park had been engineered so that it was almost impossible for kids to hurt themselves. In spite of these safety measures, it seemed as though the adults were unable to let the kids explore and play on their own. Parents hovered and stayed very close to their children.

One mother monitored every move of her toddler on a very mundane, very short, and very boring slide. Another parent stood beside her son as he sat and played with the vertical bars of a bridge connecting a slide and its steps. She literally guided her child's hand on each bar of the bridge. Did she think he was incapable of determining where to place his hand next? Did it even matter? He was seated on the bridge. Maybe she thought he could somehow contort his body, slide between the bars and experience a disaster. Where was the freedom for these children to explore and use their imaginations? Where was the freedom for these children to succeed or fail?

Maybe you think that the playground is a very trivial example, but I'm wondering if perhaps it might be a microcosm of life. The toddler who is prevented from experiencing failure and success on the playground may become the child who is rescued and protected beyond what is reasonable and healthy. These playground kids would have learned more about themselves, explored more, and had more fun if their parents would have been close by, but not hovering.

But, John, what about safety? Is there a guarantee that a child will not skin her knee or bump her lip if allowed to have more independence? No, there is no guarantee. But the choice to allow failure and success is worth the possibility of an occasional skinned knee or bloody lip. Mom or Dad, you can put on a little ointment and a Band-Aid or wash off that lip. The wonderful, appropriate freedom that you give your child is priceless. Your child will learn what to do and what not to do. She'll learn about the wonders of the slide and the perils of the vertical bars on the bridge. She will undoubtedly conquer some fears and revel in her victories.

How do our children gain wisdom? They grow and mature and develop as the result of success and failure. When they fail, we pick them up, dust them off, and help them understand what went wrong. When they succeed, we rejoice with them and enjoy their excitement.

Choose
to Pray

There have been times in my life when a concept or a phrase or a sentence from a spoken message has emblazoned itself in my memory. One of those times was at a church conference several years ago. The pastor delivering the morning devotion began by saying, "I want to share the outline of my message with you before I begin. My opening point is Jesus. My next point will be Jesus. And my final point, Jesus." Jesus, Jesus, Jesus. *He* was the backbone, the outline of the three-point sermon. Pastor Jack Kaley had clearly defined his path and, as my mother used to say, had "the accent on the right syllable." He was prepared to emphasize what was truly important.

All that to say, as we turn to the final choice for intentional parenting, let me begin by sharing with you all five action steps. Yes, that's right. You get a peek at all five from the very start. Step 1: Pray; Step 2: Pray; Step 3: Pray; Step 4: Pray; and Step 5: (You guessed it . . .) Pray. Is that redundant? Yes, it is. Does it "put the accent on the right syllable"? That's the idea.

STEP ❶ *Pray.*

> *"What other nation is so great as to have their gods near them the way the LORD our God is near us whenever we pray to him?"*
> —Deuteronomy 4:7

Pray Early

My dear friend and I sat in the front of the church after the service had ended. It had been a very bad week for this friend. She was recently separated from her abusive husband. She was struggling emotionally, financially, and in almost every other category you can name. As she poured out the details of the past few days, we wept together. My mind raced as I attempted to find a solution or at least a suggestion to the myriad of problems she had listed. I sat in silence as nothing came to mind. She glanced at my troubled face and somehow knew I was straining to find a practical answer to her dilemma. She also knew that there was no logical solution, no quick fix. "I guess all we can do is pray," she said amid the tears.

When she spoke those words, we looked at one another simultaneously and laughed. *All* we can do is pray? Had that just come out of her mouth? Had I momentarily agreed that prayer was, indeed, our last resort? Our temporary lack of faith, and our realization that prayer had somehow been relegated to the final answer, was shocking. But that shock opened my eyes. Prayer must be my *first* resort. Pray early. Step 1: Pray; and then be sure to . . .

STEP ❷ *Pray.*

> *"Pray continually."*
> —1 Thessalonians 5:17

Pray Often

There have been various times in my life when my sleep has been interrupted. The first time I remember this happening on a regular basis was when I was six months pregnant with our first child. There are only a limited number of comfortable resting positions when you are in the kind of shape I was in. I could fall asleep, but I didn't stay asleep. So after Matthew was born, I looked forward to a full night's sleep. (You already know where I'm going, don't you?) Neither Matthew, nor his brother Aaron, nor their brother Jonathan slept through the night at a young age. My nighttime interruptions continued until the youngest son was over a year old. By the time this happened, I had two children in school.

Then I enjoyed more peaceful sleep (not counting the few bouts of nighttime illness). Perhaps this is where you are today, basking in your uninterrupted eight hours each night and imagining that this bliss will continue forever. You believe that you have reached the light at the end of the tunnel. I hate to be the bearer of bad news, but . . . don't count on it! It's possible that the light you see is the headlights of a teenager's car.

Slumber parties, youth group, socializing, ball games, driver's licenses—need I say more? And when that season of life is over, you find yourself waking up "just because."

One night recently, at about 2:07 a.m., I was wide awake, just because, and wondering how long it would take before I fell asleep once again. By 3:11 a.m., I was still not in dreamland, so out of frustration, I came up with a plan. If I wasn't going to be sound asleep, at least I could take comfort in the fact that I was in an *attitude* of sleep. I was in a horizontal position on my bed, my eyes and lips were closed, and my pillow was fluffed just right. I might not be asleep, but I was in an attitude of sleep.

Maybe you've heard something like this someplace else. "Please be in an attitude of prayer," the pastor says. Most of us know what that means. You are to close your eyes, fold your hands, and bow your head. That is the attitude of prayer . . . right?

The question I want to pose is, Does an attitude of prayer indicate that prayer is taking place? No, not any more than an attitude of sleep means I'm sleeping. Prayer is not based on posture. Prayer is communication with your heavenly Father.

The freedom from a preferred posture is why we are able to obey the Lord's instruction to "pray continually" (1 Thessalonians 5:17). We are not required to have head bowed, eyes closed, and hands folded. We can have a God-consciousness, all the time, without ceasing. Can you see how continual prayer could transform your words, your actions, your decisions, your thoughts? If Christ was on your mind at all times, He would obviously influence each word, each action, each decision, each thought. That is His desire. Pray often.

Let's recap. Step 1: Pray; Step 2: Pray; and now on to Step 3 . . .

STEP ❸ *Pray.*

> *"As for me, far be it from me that I should sin against the LORD by failing to pray for you."*
> —1 Samuel 12:23

Pray for Yourself

It is neither arrogant nor unimportant to pray for yourself. God encourages us to do just that. "If any of you lacks wisdom, he should ask God, who gives generously to all without finding fault, and it will be given to him" (James 1:5). Mom or Dad, do you need wisdom in your parenting? Undoubtedly the answer is yes. God wants you to ask Him.

Why do we hesitate to ask God? Perhaps it is because we don't want to know the answer. If I ask God for wisdom and He reveals something seemingly unpleasant that *I* must do, someway that I must change *my* behavior or attitude, I'm not sure I want to hear it. God will definitely reveal wisdom to those who ask, but the change in behavior is our choice.

Another possible reason we fail to ask God for wisdom is we "tried that once and it didn't work." Huh? There's something wrong with that picture. If something God has promised seems not to work, the problem is not with God. Perhaps the issue is timing. We live in a world where *instant* is not always fast enough. Our messaging is instant. Our oatmeal is instant. Our digital photo review is instant. If we can enjoy the quick and painless in all those avenues, why doesn't God give us wisdom just as quickly? My best guess is that He gives us wisdom when it is best for us to

123

have wisdom. I love the analogy of this told by Corrie ten Boom, a girl who was accustomed to riding the train with her father.

> Father sat down on the edge of the narrow bed. "Corrie," he began gently, "when you and I go to Amsterdam— when do I give you your ticket?"
>
> I sniffed a few times considering this. "Why, just before we get on the train."
>
> "Exactly. And our wise Father in heaven knows when we're going to need things, too. Don't run out ahead of Him, Corrie."[1]

If you ask, God will give you wisdom when you need it. Ask. Listen. Don't rush the Holy Spirit. And be prepared to follow the wisdom given, whether or not it makes you uncomfortable.

Pray for Your Spouse

John is one of my favorite people in the whole world. I would rather spend time with him than with anyone else. (I wish I could bottle and sell that kind of attraction.) My tried-and-true comment when someone shares a compliment about John with me is, "I don't deserve him, but I do appreciate him. And that goes a long way."

I love and appreciate John, and yet I haven't always been consistent in lifting him up in prayer. When I have failed to do this, I have missed the most important thing I could do to show my love and appreciation for him.

Books have been written about how to pray for your spouse. People who are much more learned than I have devoted page after page to encouragement and help in this area. What can I add to that plethora of information? Let me suggest a plan that will make praying for your spouse an easier task. It worked for me.

Choose an edifying verse of Scripture. Pray that verse every day for one month.

> For example, 3 John 2:
> *"Dear friend, I pray that you may enjoy good health and that all may go well with you, even as your soul is getting along well."*
> Now insert your spouse's name:
> *I pray that John will prosper and be in good health, and that all may go well with him, even as his soul is getting along well.*

The blessing received by praying the Word of God is twofold. You are praying for your spouse and you are repeating the Word of God. His Word is becoming a part of your daily routine and memory. When you have finished a month of one Scripture prayer, choose another passage. Such as . . .

> Philippians 4:6:
> *I pray that John will not be "anxious about anything, but in everything, by prayer and petition, with thanksgiving, will present [his] requests to God."*

Pray for Your Child

As we read in James 5:16: "The prayer of a righteous man is powerful and effective." I once heard someone say,

"When I get to heaven and learn just how powerful and effective prayer was, I will wish I had prayed more." Do not miss the opportunity to pray for your child. What sorts of things do you pray for? I recommend you pray for wisdom. When your son or daughter is able to discern right from wrong, able to make a good choice instead of a poor choice, that is wisdom. And, of course, choosing to follow Jesus is the very best choice.

Pray that God will give your child *courage*. Sometimes wisdom is not enough. Courage is needed in order to carry out the insight gained through wisdom. It takes courage to stand apart from the crowd when the crowd is moving in the wrong direction. It takes courage to trust the Word when people all around are encouraging what is disobedient to it.

Courage is not lack of fear. Courage is fear rightly placed. It is appropriate and positive to fear the Lord. In simple terms, fearing God indicates that you believe He is real and that His instructions are not to be ignored. In parental terms, God is not speaking to you through His Word "just to hear His head roar." Pray that your child will have courage and be obedient to the instructions of the Lord.

Pray for wisdom. Pray for courage. And pray for intervention in the *concerns of your child's life*. Those concerns will change greatly as your child matures. Your toddler might have a scratch or a scrape that needs your prayers. Your preschooler might need prayer for her friend in Sunday school. Your elementary age child may have a concern that is related to school . . . his performance, his understanding, or maybe his relationship with other students or her teacher. Pray for the concerns on your child's heart. And remember, too, to pray for your child's *protection*.

Whose Will?

Not too long ago I was very aware that one of my sons needed prayer. He was going through a difficult situation, and he needed divine wisdom, courage, intervention, and protection. I pleaded with the Lord to do what *I* was sure was in this son's best interest. Did I *ask* what was best for my child? No, I didn't want to ask, because I didn't want the answer to be different from what I had determined was best. Then one morning right after I was done praying, in essence, that *my* will be done, I sensed the still, small voice of the Lord. "Kendra, did you forget that I love him more than you do?" Yes, I had forgotten. I stopped in my tracks, repented of my arrogance, and prayed for the Lord's will to be done in the life of my child. I know that His will is the best. In fact, it is perfect.

Pray for Others

One of the greatest privileges you have is to pray for someone. Besides praying for yourself, your spouse, and your child, there are others who can benefit from your intervention. In our church we have a time each week when the congregation shares joys and concerns. If that is true in your church, take time to jot down what is said. If you don't take note of the concerns, it will be very difficult to remember them later in the week. You can write them on the church bulletin and then put that on your refrigerator when you arrive home. The list is there to remind you and others in the family to pray for the needs expressed. You might even pray for one or two of the concerns each evening at your dinner prayer. By demonstrating your interest in the needs of others in your church family, you are modeling that for your children.

One of the things I wish we had done when our children were little was to sponsor a Compassion International child. That wonderful organization provides people with the opportunity to give of their finances and their prayers to less fortunate children around the globe. Today John and I sponsor a little girl named Joilan in the Dominican Republic. Her picture is on our refrigerator, and she is on my daily list of prayer concerns. It would have been a wonderful lesson for our kids to be introduced to a Compassion child when they were only children themselves. Consider sponsoring a child and illustrating to your children the global reality of physical and spiritual needs that your family can pray about.

Remember the steps we have covered. Step 1: Pray; Step 2: Pray; Step 3: Pray; and . . .

STEP ❹ *Pray.*

> *"Again, I tell you that if two of you on earth agree about anything you ask for, it will be done for you by my Father in heaven. For where two or three come together in my name, there am I with them."*
> —Matthew 18:19–20

Pray with Your Spouse

We already talked about praying for your spouse. This is the suggestion to pray *with* your spouse. You know the importance of being on the same team and singing off the same song sheet in parenting. Nothing will facilitate that more than praying together.

The biggest roadblock to a couple praying together is getting started. "When should we pray together? How should we pray together?" Those are the two questions most frequently asked. There is not one specific answer to either of them. Let me give you some ideas of what has worked in our home and in the homes of others.

> ON AVERAGE, CHRISTIAN PARENTS PRAY WITH THEIR SPOUSE ONLY ONCE A WEEK.

When?

As newlyweds, I was certain that John and I had been wired with internal clocks that were in opposition to one another. He was an "early to bed, early to rise" kind of guy, and I preferred to burn the midnight oil. One way is not right and one way wrong, but if you and your spouse have different internal clocks, you have eliminated two of the most convenient times to join together in prayer . . . before going to sleep or when you first wake up.

My nocturnal ways became impractical when our children reached school age. Part of my responsibility involved early morning duties. Making the transition was not easy, but it was necessary. (Another reminder of an earlier action step: It wasn't all about me.) I recall telling John how hard it was to get up early in the morning. I also remember his reply. "You don't have a problem getting up. You have a problem going to bed." Point well-taken. My shift from late riser to earlier riser has given us time together at both ends of the day . . . time together to pray.

If neither late night nor early morning will work for you and your spouse, talk about when you can come together in prayer. Be flexible. If breakfast time is better for the two of you, great! When you are choosing a time, remember that you will want to have very few, if any, interruptions. Keep your goal in mind—it is to pray with your spouse. Do what you can do to discover when this prayer time is best for the two of you.

How?

Praying together often requires that you dialogue in preparation. Start your prayer time with conversation. I suggest you discuss the concerns you have about your child. What parenting problems and circumstances have developed recently? What answers have you seen to previous prayer? Communication with your spouse (or preparation for prayer) is a very important aspect of *how* to pray. It is through this communication that you can arrive at agreement. Then from your agreement, you can offer your requests, your intercession, and your praise to God together. If one of you is more comfortable praying aloud, let that spouse take the lead. The other spouse should feel free to chime in at any time but should not feel pressured to do so. The longer you pray together, the more comfortable each of you will become. John and I like to hold hands when we pray together, but remember what we learned about the *attitude* of prayer. It is not your posture; it is your heart. Praying with your spouse is important and it is a choice.

Pray with Your Child

Pray for *and* with your child. This is a little easier to co-ordinate than praying with your spouse, especially if you are starting when your son or daughter is young. The routine you establish for praying together will be your child's "normal."

When?

Let's begin by talking about *when* to pray. You have many choices and do not have to limit your prayer time to once a day. You can start the day together in prayer. You can pray with your child at bedtime. Mealtime is another time to pray together. Undoubtedly, special concerns will surface during the day—take advantage of those times too. Every bump and bruise, every scratch and scrape can move you to prayer. A day or two after asking God to heal a shin that was bleeding, be sure to thank Him for the scab that has formed and for His healing of the wound.

ON AVERAGE, CHRISTIAN PARENTS PRAY WITH THEIR CHILD ONLY THREE OUT OF SEVEN DAYS A WEEK.

When your children are school age, unless homeschooled, they are gone several hours each day. This is a good time to solidify a specific time to pray together. We prayed with our children in the morning after breakfast. We prayed with each child individually at bedtime until the kids reached the age where they chose to pray independently. Be prepared to change the routine, the *when* of your prayers, as the situation changes. By the way, when your children are at school, let them know that you will be praying for them throughout the day and remind them that they can pray too!

How?

As the parent, you will likely take the lead initially in praying with your child. You can ask your son or daughter what they would like you to include in your prayer. "Do you have anyone special you want to pray for? Is there anything going on that we need to pray about?" You may be surprised what is on your child's heart. Remember *nothing* that your child considers important should be deemed unimportant. Let him add names and circumstances so that he has ownership of the prayers. Many times, my husband or I would add the name of a friend or relative at the prompting of our child, only to later discover that a need had existed.

Keep your vocabulary simple and appropriate for the age of your child. The goals of this prayer time together are many. Prayer is becoming a regular part of his life. You are teaching him that prayer is not an exercise in futility but communication with his loving heavenly Father. Prayer is a privilege. You are communicating your love for both your child and for the Lord by taking the time to pray together. And you are investing in the prayer life of your before-you-know-it adult child. The *when* and *how* with your child are important, but it is so much more important to (in the words of Nike) just do it!

Let's recap. Step 1: Pray; Step 2: Pray; Step 3: Pray; Step 4: Pray; and finally . . .

STEP ❺ *Pray.*

"If my people, who are called by my name, will humble themselves and pray and seek my face and turn from their wicked ways, then will I hear from heaven and will forgive their sin and will heal their land."
—2 Chronicles 7:14

As we come to this final action step of the final choice, I am struggling to present a powerful, persuasive plea to you to pray, pray, pray. Do I tell you of yet one more time when prayer was powerful in my life? Do I direct you to books on prayer by noted theologians and well-known authors? Do I quote Scripture on the importance and privilege of prayer? No, I have determined that the best thing I can do is to pause and pray for you. I don't know your name or your child's name. I don't know your circumstances or your situation, but I do know your heavenly Father. Let's pray.

Father, I come to You today and intercede on behalf of the reader of this book. The trials, challenges, and joys of being the parent are many. You know the needs of this family. And You love this reader and his or her child more than words could possibly express. I pray that You will meet their needs.

Your Word promises that we can ask for wisdom and You will give it. Give this parent wisdom, in child rearing and in other aspects of life. Grant the grace necessary to be a positive role model. Encourage him or her to be an encourager, to be present, to discipline in love, and to allow failure and success. In short, help this reader to be a godly parent.

Thank You, Lord, for being the parent to all who call upon You in faith. Thank You for being accessible and for enjoying fellowship with Your children. Thank You for the privilege of praying this prayer together.

In Your Son's precious name, the name of Jesus, amen.

ACTION STEPS:

STEP ❶ Pray.

STEP ❷ Pray.

STEP ❸ Pray.

STEP ❹ Pray.

STEP ❺ Pray.

A Good Word from John —The Resident Dad

There have been many books written about how to pray, when to pray, and the different kinds of prayer. These can be helpful tools. Even the disciples, the men who actually walked with Jesus, needed help when it came to prayer. They went straight to Him. "One day Jesus was praying in a certain place. When

*he finished, one of his disciples said to him, 'Lord,
teach us to pray'" (Luke 11:1).*

Prayer in its simplest form is talking with God. It
is a natural result of loving Him, trusting Him, and
seeking His kingdom before all else. Jesus didn't have
difficulty with prayer. He loved His heavenly Father,
trusted Him, and was diligent to seek first the kingdom of God and to do His will. That made prayer
natural and necessary for Jesus. He took every opportunity to pray. As we love the Lord, trust Him,
and long to do His will, we will also find conversing
with God natural and necessary.

Our family went on vacation to the East Coast
one summer. While in Philadelphia, we stopped at a
grocery store to get some supplies. The boys and I
stayed in the car and Kendra went in to do the shopping. As she exited the car, one of the boys smiled
and hollered, "Don't visit with anyone you don't
know!" You see, our kids knew their mom. Kendra
enjoys visiting with people. That includes longtime
friends and new friends she might meet at the grocery store in Philadelphia. She loves to talk with
people and to get to know them.

That is how natural prayer should be. We should
simply enjoy talking with God and getting to know
Him better. Prayer isn't just asking for things. Prayer
isn't just a discipline. Prayer isn't all about you or
me; it's all about God. Prayer is connecting with the
Lord and keeping Him first in our lives. Prayer can be
as natural and delightful as Kendra visiting with an
old friend or a new one, over a cup of tea or in the
grocery store in Philadelphia.

And prayer is necessary. It isn't easy to Be The

Parent. We need help. We need our heavenly Father's help. Love Him. Trust Him. Seek the kingdom of God first. And pray continually.

Note:
1. Corrie ten Boom with John and Elizabeth Sherrill, *The Hiding Place* (Carmel, N.Y.: Guideposts, 1971), 33.

# Conclusion

What do you want to be when you grow up?" Do you remember hearing that question as a child? You probably heard the same question in high school and maybe even in college (especially from your parents if you changed your major more than once). "What do you want to be?"

We typically answer that question with the career field that interests us. My answer was always, "I want to be a teacher." After I had been married for several years and taught school the majority of those years, my answer became, "I want to be a mom." And that is what happened when I became pregnant and gave birth to our first child. That's how it happens for the majority of moms and dads. They become Mom and Dad when their child is born. For others, the transition to Mom or Dad occurs with adoption.

As lengthy and difficult as the adoption process might be, or as painful and extended as your labor and delivery might have been, becoming a mom or dad is not the ultimate challenge. The challenge, the charge from God, is to Be The Parent. Those three words suggest a great privilege, a great opportunity, and a great responsibility. The purpose of this book has been to equip you for the task and to encourage you along the way.

If you will diligently make the seven choices you have been presented with and apply the five action steps of each choice, you will be on your way to raising great kids! And what is a great kid? Someone who loves God, who obeys God, and who glorifies God in what he does. What a blessing your great kids can be . . . to God, to you, and to our world! Take the challenge. Make the choice. Be The Parent.

Appendix:
The Plan
of Salvation

Ask God to speak to you as you read the following Scriptures:

- Romans 3:23—All have sinned.

- Romans 6:23—Eternal life is a free gift of God.

- Romans 5:8—Because of love, Jesus paid the death penalty for your sins.

- Romans 10:9–10—Confess Jesus as Lord and believe God raised Him from the dead.

- Romans 10:13—Ask God to save you and He will.

To place your faith in Jesus and receive His gift of eternal life, you must:

- Recognize that God created you for a love relationship with Him. He wants you to love Him with all your being.

- Recognize that you are a sinner and you cannot save yourself.

- Believe that Jesus paid a death penalty for your sin by His death on the cross and rose from the dead in victory over death.

- Confess (agree with God about) your sins that separate you from Him.

- Repent of your sins (turn from sin to God).

- Ask Jesus to save you by His grace (undeserved favor).

- Turn over the rule in your life to Jesus. Let Him be your Lord.

If you have just made this important decision, call someone and share the good news of what God has done in your life. Then share your decision with your church.

Source:
Henry T. Blackaby and Claude V. King, *Experiencing God* (Nashville: Broadman and Holman, 1994), 2.

LIVE LIFE INENTIONALLY!
This phrase describes Kendra's
life and the message that she brings
to her listening and reading audiences.
Kendra would be delighted to hear from you.
Contact her at: www.KendraSmiley.com

More from Kendra Smiley and Moody Publishers!

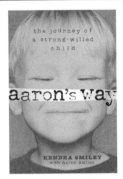

Aaron's Way
the journey of a strong-willed child

ISBN: 0-8024-4349-4
ISBN-13: 978-0-8024-4349-6

When Kendra Smiley gave birth to her second son, she told the doctor, "Oh, good! I already know how to do boys!" Twenty years later she laughs at her own naiveté. Aaron Joseph Smiley was born with a mind of his own. *Aaron's Way* will help stressed-out parents realize that:

• You are not alone

• The strong-willed child has thought and behavior patterns that can be understood and anticipated

• There are insights and strategies that can help you and your child on the journey.

If you are struggling with raising a strong-willed child, this book is a must-read. As author Julie Ann Barnhill says, "You'll laugh, nod your head madly in agreement, and perhaps, like me, find yourself racing to the side of your own 'Aaron' and whispering a prayer of thanks for this one so uniquely created."